IMPERIAL WAR MUSEUM REVIEW

ARTICLES ON ASPECTS OF
TWENTIETH CENTURY HISTORY
PRINCIPALLY BY THE STAFF OF
THE IMPERIAL WAR MUSEUM

PUBLISHED BY
THE TRUSTEES OF
THE IMPERIAL WAR MUSEUM
GENERAL EDITOR:
SUZANNE BARDGETT
HISTORICAL EDITOR:
PETER SIMKINS
COVER DESIGN BY
GRUNDY & NORTHEDGE DESIGNERS
PRINTED BY
GRILLFORD
© TRUSTEES OF THE IMPERIAL
WAR MUSEUM AND THE AUTHORS 1994
BRITISH LIBRARY CATALOGUING-IN-PUBLICATION DATA
A CATALOGUE RECORD FOR THIS BOOK IS AVAILABLE
FROM THE BRITISH LIBRARY
ISBN 1 870423 14 3

Cover illustration: *Volunteer helpers distributing tea to victims of the Blitz. Reproduced by kind permission of George Rodger*

Contents

George Rodger: gentleman, traveller, and photographer

Jane Carmichael

Jane Carmichael is Keeper of the Department of Photographs.

To meet George Rodger today is to meet a distinguished white-haired gentleman in his eighties, who recalls a long and adventurous life with precision and gusto. Sitting in his Kent garden, enjoying some excellent red wine on a summer afternoon, he looked back over the years and recalled with a dry wit some of the excitements and challenges he faced as a photographer in wartime and in the succeeding decades. Rodger has never been a man to seek personal fame, but this year, 1994, has seen his work achieve a high profile with a retrospective exhibition at the Royal Photographic Society, numerous profiles in the press and an honorary fellowship from the Society in recognition of his personal achievement as a documentary photographer and his contribution towards the recognition of the status of the profession.

Born in Hale, Cheshire in 1908, into a family of Scottish merchants, George Rodger was just over thirty at the start of the Second World War. His taste for roving had already led him to join the Merchant Navy at eighteen, to try tea planting in Assam, to survive during the Depression in a variety of odd jobs in the United States, and finally back to England in 1936, to find himself a job as a photographic assistant at the embryonic television studios of the BBC. He soon found more of interest outside the studio, left the BBC and, at the outbreak of war, was working as a freelance for a photographic agency, 'Black Star.' He began to submit more and more of his work to the prestigious American photo magazine *Life* and by mid-1940 had built up a satisfactory, if precarious, relationship as one of its London suppliers or 'stringers.'

At this stage his photography was largely a means to an end; it allowed him to maintain his independence and brought him opportunities for travel and adventure. However, in the course of the war, through his connection with *Life,* first as freelance and then, from October 1942 onwards, as a full time staff photographer, he came to occupy a position different from that of any other British photographer. Unlike the usual 'official' man with the forces – the professional photographer recruited or conscripted for public relations purposes – he was never formally part of any military organisation nor subject to its hierarchy. Neither did he attempt to follow the pack of professional photographers and journalists visiting the various theatres of war for relatively brief periods. His work was subject to the usual military censorship, but he preferred to follow his own bent, to travel as he saw fit, to observe whatever struck him of interest, to document events carefully in his diaries and notes, and never to impose himself on any situation but to let the image speak for itself in the eye of his camera. This quiet, understated but informative style resulted in a formidable body of work taken during the war years. It ranged from Britain to Africa, to the Far East and Europe. It documented the nature of war from the devastation of the Blitz to the horrors of Belsen, and from the fighting in Eritrea to the fall of Rangoon and the surrender of Germany. At the same time it prefigured the direction his photography would take in the decades after the war; he found he was drawn to the observation and portrayal of the primitive societies in Africa and the Far East. The war years established George Rodger as a photographer of extraordinary abilities and experience. In a rare personal profile of one of its staff in 1942 *Life* gave him an eight page 'spread' entitled *75,000 Miles* and announced that 'George Rodger has gone to more sweat and pain to get pictures than any other *Life* photographer.' [1] Typically, Rodger fled New York the week the issue appeared after too much casual recognition in the street.

Throughout the war, *Life* magazine had a reciprocal agreement with the Ministry of Information in London, so that the work of its photographers could be circulated in Europe. Gradually George Rodger's work on wartime Britain was used more and more, albeit anonymously, in the staple British picture magazines of the period, *Picture Post* and *Illustrated*. During 1939 and 1940 he covered the home front in Britain, catching the nuances of mood, from the anti-climax of the first few months, the resilience of children finding adventure in the shelters, the surviving glamour and intensity of London's night life in cellar bars and nightclubs, as well as the untiring efforts of firefighters, ARP wardens and others after the nights of bombing.

However, at the end of 1940 George Rodger looked for wider horizons. *Life* were prepared to give him a roving assignment in the current main theatre of war, Africa, and he found he could arrange accreditation to the Free French Forces. In Africa his capacity for survival was to be tested to the limit. Simply getting to the theatre of war presented difficulties which would have daunted a lesser man. His sea voyage took him in a vast semi-circle out into the Atlantic ocean from Glasgow to land in French Cameroon. From there, undeterred by the deserts and mountains that lay in his way, he proposed to set out first northwards across French West Africa towards Koufra, Mussolini's staging post to his East African conquests which was under French siege, then eastwards

George Rodger in the doorway of one his less salubrious billets in the Western Desert, 1941. E 3952E

across the Sudan to Eritrea and Somaliland where Free French Forces were engaged with British, Indian and Sudanese in driving the occupying Italian army out. He teamed up with the 'Baron', a French interpreter who:

> …was an obscure sort of a person who owned a gold mine somewhere and who wore the buttons of the Foreign Legion on his self-designed, oatmeal-coloured, linen uniform. …he had the most virulent temper and a passion for statistics. But also he had a genuine and intimate knowledge of the whole of the Camerouns and French Equatorial Africa, and knew every planter and trader and government official between Brazzaville and Fort Lamy. [2]

Equipped with 46 pieces of luggage, mostly the Baron's, and a Chevrolet truck and the Baron's own Oldsmobile, *La Mission de Reportage* as it had been dubbed, set out northwards. The 'Baron' proved to be a tower of strength provided that the current plan suited him. They survived frequent breakdowns, natural hazards of heat and cold, uncharted routes in '*région sans eau et sans vegetation*' but 'give the Baron another Frenchman of suitable standing with whom to talk and drink with' and he was impossible to prise away for any journalistic consideration. Koufra fell to the Free French on 1 March 1941 but much to

The proprietor of the Hungaria nightclub serves breakfast to guests who have been offered and accepted nightclothes and accommodation during a raid.

Rodger's chagrin, *La Mission de Reportage* did not arrive until the following day. Nevertheless, having taken some photographs, Rodger and the Baron started their journey eastwards towards Eritrea a few days later. Conditions were appalling:

> It was impossible to get out of first gear in the deep sand, and to drive for more than ten minutes without having to get out and dig was a holy miracle. It took three days working from sun-up to sunset, to cover one hundred miles. [3]

However, their courage and perseverance brought them through to Eritrea as the Italian forces around Massawa collapsed. Busy photographing the Allied attack, Rodger had become isolated when suddenly:

> ...I found myself face to face with five Italians advancing up a wadi towards me, their rifles at the ready, and their short, blunt bayonets shining dully in the sun. Undoubtedly, I

thought, this must be the time to surrender. After all, I had nothing to defend myself with and they were less than ten yards away. I was unaccustomed to surrendering to Italians and was not sure of the conventional things to do, and anyway, I did not want to drop my camera in the sand. So, what with one thing and another, I took so long that they beat me to it and surrendered first. [4]

Rodger often came up against the recurrent problem of his unorthodox status; at this stage he was a British photographer accredited to the Free French Forces working for an American magazine. Although the British Ministry of Information had the use of his pictures through the reciprocal arrangement with *Life*, the War Office was not prepared to offer the support of the Army Public Relations units, apparently on the grounds that it had already accredited one *Life* representative, James Jarché, to the African theatre. Much depended on Rodger's success with contacts at the local level. Despairing of army support when he finally arrived at

Machine gunners of the Foreign Legion in action during the battle of Massawa.

Cairo headquarters, he left his unexposed films for development and transmission with the British Embassy. In a calamitous encounter with an Egyptian photographer organised by the Embassy and of which he was unaware until later, most of the negatives of his African journeys were ruined. Rodger wrote dryly: 'I had sweated across 9000 miles of Africa to get those pictures. It was a little annoying.' [5]

From Cairo, having separated from the Baron, Rodger travelled to Abyssinia and then on to Syria where British and Free French Forces were trying to defeat the forces of Vichy France. As usual Rodger's eagerness to get photographs led to danger, this time on the road to Damascus:

> ...I saw the planes returning. They zoomed down to only double the height of the telegraph poles along the roadside and opened up with their machine-guns, spattering the sand around us with angry little spurts of dust. I prayed. I guess we all did. I thought we were all as good as dead, and my

mouth went horribly dry. But I thought I might as well get some more pictures of our finale and decided to leap up as the next plane went over the top and grab a quick picture as it flew away. ...I lay as flat as I could get to the ground and could almost feel the draught as it roared over me. Then I leaped up to get my picture, and immediately froze in horror. I was unable even to raise my camera. For a fraction of a second I looked the rear gunner straight in the eye... I was so astonished, I just stood there paralysed and let him shoot at me. [6]

After the defeat of the Vichy forces in Syria on 8 June 1941, Rodger decided to make for Iran where the British and Russian forces were advancing from north and south to occupy the country. Obviously the moment of their meeting would be a tremendous occasion and, as usual, it required all Rodger's initiative and disregard of the formalities of the official press party to get to the right place. He travelled most of the way in a taxi with an

Children in an air raid shelter.

enthusiastic if dare-devil Iraqi driver. 'George'. On 25 August they caught up with the advance armour brigade due to rendezvous with the Russians, 'George's' panache took them right to the front of the column of British vehicles where they saw:

> ...the first of the Russians [armoured cars] but as we approached it, its two-pounder gun swivelled round and came to rest pointing directly at us. We hoped that whoever was behind it, would recognise the Union Jack before he pulled the trigger. Then, as we drew nearer, the turret opened and a Russian corporal climbed out. The Brigadier shook him by the hand. The first contact between the British and Russian forces had been made, and I was the only one to photograph it... For all we knew the press party sent out officially by the Middle East was still somewhere in Southern Iran. [7]

After spending some time with the occupying forces, Rodger travelled briefly to India and its north-west frontier to see the frontiers of Empire. But November saw the renewal of the campaign in the Western Desert and he rejoined the forces there to find himself celebrating Christmas with other correspondents in Benghazi, which had fallen to the Allies on Christmas Eve.

Life headquarters in New York decided that Rodger should travel next to Burma where the British were crumbling before the Japanese onslaught. By February 1942 Rodger was watching and taking pictures as the city of Rangoon was engulfed in flames. The country suffered greatly as the Japanese advanced and on 1 May 1942 Mandalay surrendered. In powerful prose Rodger described the devastated city just before the end:

> Mandalay, that proud city, once the capital of the Kingdom of Ava, steeped in tradition, now lay a heap of smouldering ruins. Blue-grey wisps of smoke still rose from acres of piled ashes where once the business and the native sections stood. The entire district was utterly destroyed and all that remained of Mandalay was the stench of her dead that lay beneath the ruins. Charred bodies sprawled in the streets and rotting corpses floated among the lily-pads in the moat surrounding the rose-red walls of Fort Dufferin, the inner city of ancient Mandalay....A fire-blackened pagoda still raised its spire as though in defiance from the smoking cinders, and trees, white with

Russian and British officers meet in Iran, 25 August 1941.

ash, lifted their smouldering limbs in supplication to the sky....Every temple had gone; the bazaars and the shops had gone, and the homes of 150,000 people; Mandalay itself had gone. What took a thousand years to build took but an hour to fall. [8]

It was rare for Rodger in his wanderings through desert or jungle to have many encounters with 'top brass' but whenever he did, he made the most of the occasion. Not only was the result usually a successful photograph, but often a lengthy conversation as well, as Rodger's perception and understanding made him at ease with the upper echelons. In Burma the opportunity arose to photograph a meeting at Maymyo in Burma between Generalissimo Chiang Kai-shek, the leader of nationalist China which was supporting Burma, his influential and attractive wife, Madame Chiang, and the American Lieutenant-General Joseph Stilwell, Commander of all Chinese forces. Rodger found Madame Chiang had matters well in hand:

> When they [the Generalissimo and Madame Chiang] came down the steps, 'Uncle Joe'

Rangoon in flames, February 1942. JAR 1258

Stilwell was with them. I thought I would probably have to pose them, but Madame Chiang knew exactly what kind of picture I wanted even before I asked. The 'Entente Cordiale' picture she called it as she placed herself between the Generalissimo and 'Uncle Joe', and took their arms, smiling into camera. ...she kept the conversation going in a flippant strain to give me a variety of expressions and to help 'Uncle Joe' relax a little. It was obvious he would rather face a battery of guns than a camera. [9]

But in his journeys to and fro in Burma it was the civilian victims of war and the inherent beauty of the country and its people which attracted his camera. Burma had a large resident labour force of Indians. They were now the poorest of the refugees from the fallen cities and, as aliens, were subject to hostility and exploitation rather than sympathy. Rodger watched at the roadside to record their migration, and their obvious fears of what had been and what was to come:

They were without shelter and without food, and much of the money they had been able to bring with them had been squeezed out of them by the Burmans in the villages through which they had passed...As we went further south, the bands of refugees became thicker on the road until we found them straggling northwards in a continual stream. There must have been 50,000 to 60,000 of them. Dock labourers, coolies, and bearers plodded side by side with clerks and government servants, their womenfolk and children trailing beside them. In endless streams they came- women tired out and hobbling along by the aid of sticks; men carrying babies slung in panniers from their shoulders, others carrying small children on their backs. [10]

The hallmark of Rodger's later portraits and studies of primitive people – and their unselfconsciousness before his camera – emerged very strongly in photographs taken in the Shan states and Naga hills. He found:

> ...the quaintest little Shan villages, some of which looked like stage sets for a costume play. The back cloth was of green twisted jungle. The props were mostly little Shan houses with balconies, and a bench or a well outside, around which the players grouped themselves in picturesque natural poses. Flowers festooned the wings and costumes rivalled even the flowers in their brightness. The players all wore gay-coloured 'lungyis' and, though the men were naked to the waist, the girls wore starched white bodices, tight sleeved and sometimes pertly boleroed behind. They wore orchids in their hair, gold and silver bangles on their wrists. [11]

The Japanese advance cut him off from the conventional sea or air route back to India so with typical determination, he decided to cross the frontier over the Naga hills, an area reputedly populated by the headhunters of the Naga tribe. The roads were few and uncertain, the terrain a forbidding mixture of jungle and mountain. George Rodger set out with a fellow correspondent in two jeeps on 10 April 1942 on a journey as difficult as any he had encountered in Africa. As they pushed northwards the roads petered out altogether:

> Only a jungle track led out of Shingbwiyaung. There was no vestige of a road at all, and every few yards we had to stop and slash away bamboos with our dahs [long knives] which we had bought from the Kachins [local tribesmen]. In places trees had fallen across the pathway, bringing with them a tangle of creepers and vines. We had to cut through these with axes, and as we worked in that overpowering heat and humidity, our clothes became as wringing wet with sweat as they had been the day before from the rainfall. [12]

The terrain finally became impossible for the jeeps and

they faced walking without maps or guides the last 130 miles to the border with Assam across the high mountain ranges. On the basis of their recognition of the single word 'Ledo', the town at the railhead in Assam, they recruited some Nagas as porters and guides. The walk was a gruelling experience, not helped by the fact that the scanty tinned rations which they had been able to buy consisted of impossibly rich and unsuitable food such as paté de foie gras and cherries in brandy:

> As we slogged doggedly on hour after hour, our tired coolies now straggling out behind us, it seemed the path would never end, and our feet were so sore and swollen that we were hardly averaging one mile an hour on the uphill grades. We tried lying down whenever we stopped, to rest our muscles, but ants swarmed over us, and leeches got under our shirts, so we changed our tactics and rested whenever there was a convenient log to sit on.

Germans surrender in the Western Desert, December 1941. E 4034E

Fisherman on Inlé Lake, Shan States.

In the evenings we just collapsed, with hardly strength enough to open a can for supper. [13]

Nevertheless, they won through and in the estimation of the local planters in Assam were the first white men ever to come through over the northern Naga mountains from Burma.

Rodger completed his travels in more conventional fashion, making his way back across the world by orthodox routes and means of transport. He arrived in New York in September 1942 to be offered a position as a full time photographer for *Life*. However, for the rest of the year and well into 1943 he was occupied with recovering his health and putting two books on his wartime experiences together; *Red Moon Rising* on Burma was published in 1943, and *Desert Journey* on Africa appeared in 1944. A new dimension as a writer was added to his growing reputation as a photographer.

September 1943 saw him back in Europe working for *Life*, covering the Allied landings at Salerno in Italy. He followed the Italian campaign, then returned to Britain to accompany the long-awaited invasion of Europe on 6 June 1944. He described his arrival on the secured and relatively quiet British 'Gold' beach at Arromanches as 'a blaze of anti-climax'. [14] In many ways the campaigns in Italy and north-west Europe were the most conventional he had seen at close hand, yet he brought a fresh and remarkably sympathetic eye to the sometimes hackneyed subject of war. His photographs did not document the achievement of the conquering armies, but instead formed a compassionate record of the cost of war. He showed coffins of casualties after the relief of Naples lying in the shadow of Vesuvius awaiting burial, a dead soldier in a town street near Falaise with geraniums in bloom on the windowsill behind him, a small boy using a door as a raft to escape the floods at Walcheren. He had the searing experience of entering Belsen prison camp with the British Army in April 1945. This affected him so profoundly that he very nearly jettisoned photography altogether:

> I didn't know until then – despite over five years of war – what effect the war had had on me personally… when I discovered that I could look at the horror of Belsen – the 4,000 dead and starving lying around – and

The chief wife of the Sultan Kasser, one of the local chiefs in French West Africa.

Refugees flee Rangoon, February 1942.
JAR 1250

think only of a nice photographic composition I knew something had happened to me, and it had to stop. [15]

In the immediate post-war years Rodger found himself at something of a loss; *Life* magazine was no longer willing to allow its photographers the freedom they had previously enjoyed and he found his choice of subjects constrained. In 1947 he and some like-minded fellow photographers founded the agency Magnum, which was to be run by and for photographers, giving them control over their own work and its exploitation. All five founder members – Robert Capa, Henri Cartier-Bresson, George Rodger, David Seymour, (known as Chim) and William Vandivert – became known as the best in their field. It was through Magnum that George Rodger was able to return to Africa and work slowly and patiently with the primitive peoples there. He criss-crossed the continent several times over, consistently producing memorable work especially on the Nubas of the Sudan, the Madi of the Upper Nile, the Toureg of the Sahara and the Pygmies of the Uganda/ Congo border. He was fortunate that his maturity as a photographer coincided with the last decades of the black and white picture magazine. During the late forties and fifties television slowly eroded the status of the magazines as the main vehicle for information about the world and its more remote or exotic areas. However, the magazines were prepared to invest heavily in good material before they admitted defeat. Rodger's African essays, now regarded as his

master works, found an enthusiastic market. His patience in winning people's trust in areas where white men had hardly been and his willingness to put aside his camera until he was taken for granted, meant that he was never rejected as an intruder but rather accepted as an observer.

In 1959 Rodger finally settled in Kent in the first house he had ever owned. His travels continued albeit on a more limited scale and in the sixties and seventies he became involved with the preparation of books and exhibitions. Still active in his eighties, he is currently working on his autobiography but understandably, is finding it difficult to condense such a full life within the confines of a single book.

At the beginning of the Second World War George Rodger was an unknown adventurer who could use a camera reasonably competently. By its end he was known and respected as a courageous and shrewd photographer and writer. By remaining outside the mainstream of British official photographic effort, he had enjoyed a freedom of choice and an independence of status unknown to any other British photographer. His connection with *Life* meant that his work was given constant American and British circulation, reaching a very wide audience. Cecil Beaton was the only other British photographer who had anything like such special privileges but they were on very different terms and very much within the framework of official British photography. Neither Beaton nor Rodger recorded the narrative of war in the conventional sense but the latter's

Normal life returns; a Dutch girl prepares to clean the windows of her home.

A hill tribesman, Burma. JAR 1777

levels ensured he was the more profound observer of the two. For Beaton, the war strengthened and simplified his speciality of portraiture; for Rodger it forged him as a photographer of great range derived from his independence, patience and essential curiosity about humanity.

　　　After the war, Beaton returned to his niche in high society as its portraitist and won lasting fame as a designer of theatre, ballet, opera, musicals, and film as well as a diarist. In contrast Rodger's travels immersed him in the life of the ancient peoples of Africa. He never sought the kind of fame in which Beaton so revelled, but nonetheless has always quietly but firmly believed in the value of his work and in the importance of photographers achieving proper recognition and credit. Looking back he feels he enjoyed some privileges which have now gone forever, in particular the time and freedom to work on his chosen assignments. He feels fortunate that the span of his career coincided with the hey-day of black and white photography as a medium of mass information, but

he has also made an enormous contribution to that medium. It was indeed a lucky chance that the Second World War precipitated him into it as his chosen profession.

A small boy using a door as a raft after the flooding of Walcheren.

Notes

1. *Life* magazine, November 1942.
2. George Rodger, *Desert Journey*, Cresset Press, 1944, p 17.
3. Ibid, p 63.
4. Ibid, p 70.
5. Ibid, p 75.
6. Ibid, p 101.
7. Ibid, p 123.
8. George Rodger, *Red Moon Rising*, Cresset Press, 1943, p 98.
9. Ibid, p 99.
10. Ibid, p 63.
11. Ibid, p 109.
12. Ibid, pp 119-120.
13. Ibid, p 124.
14. *George Rodger: Magnum Opus; Fifty Years in Photojournalism*, edited by Colin Osman, text by Martin Caiger-Smith, Nishen, 1987, p 6.
15. Ibid, p 7.

Acknowledgements

I would like to thank Mr and Mrs George Rodger for the help and hospitality I enjoyed while preparing this article, and for directing me to the proper sources for the illustrations.

The Imperial War Museum Collection.

A large collection of Rodger's photographs came to the Imperial War Museum at the end of the war when the Ministry of Information made a mass transfer of material acquired for propaganda purposes. The Ministry had in turn acquired the photographs through its reciprocal arrangement with *Life* magazine whereby each could use the other's photographs. The Museum has some 100 prints derived from original negatives (E3922E – E4049E) relating to the Western Desert and approximately 350 contemporary prints of Rodger's travels in Burma (incomplete sequence JAR 1114- JAR 2227).

Further Reading

George Rodger, *Red Moon Rising*, Cresset Press, 1943.
George Rodger, *Desert Journey*, Cresset Press, 1944.
George Rodger, introduction by Inge Bondi, Gordon Fraser Photographic Monographs: 4, 1975.
George Rodger. Magnum Opus; Fifty Years in Photojournalism, edited by Colin Osman, text by Martin Caiger-Smith, Nishen, 1987.
The Blitz, the Photography of George Rodger, introduction by Tom Hopkinson, Penguin, 1990.

'A good bit of work': the Baltic diary of Commander Francis Goodhart DSO RN

Paul Kemp

Paul Kemp is a research assistant in the Department of Photographs.

At the outbreak of the First World War the submarine was a weapon of war which was unproven and whose potential was unknown. Neither the naval authorities nor the submariners themselves had any great idea of how useful their craft would be under conditions of real war as opposed to exercises. Moreover there was no body of experience on which the submariners could fall back. Early submariners literally made up the rules as they went along. They were fortunate in that the state of anti-submarine warfare was correspondingly rudimentary.

Among the papers held in the Museum's Department of Documents are the diaries of Commander Francis Goodhart DSO RN who commanded the British submarine E.8 in Home Waters and the Baltic from 1914 until December 1916 when he returned to Britain to take command of the submarine K.14 under construction at the shipyard of Fairfield & Co. at Greenock. [1]

The diaries come in two small volumes, closely filled with Goodhart's small and sometimes erratic handwriting. The style of the diaries is very fluid and they are evidently written as Goodhart would have spoken, with little in the way of punctuation. Some of the entries are very lengthy and one cannot but wonder how Goodhart managed, particularly when the submarine was at sea, when he would have had little spare time at all, to write as much as he did.

Francis Herbert Heaveningham Goodhart had joined the Royal Navy in May 1900, entered the submarine service in May 1905 and was appointed to his first command, HM Submarine C.6, on 1 September 1908. After two years' mandatory general service in the battleship HMS *Magnificent* he took command of HM Submarine D.3 in October 1912 before being appointed in command of the new submarine E.8 in 1914. In August 1914 he was one of the first British submariners to proceed to sea on the outbreak of war. Thereafter he and his crew endured the boredom and monotony of seemingly endless patrols in the Heligoland Bight where, to quote one distinguished submariner, all that they usually saw was 'water and a damn sight too much of that!'

Goodhart's command, HM Submarine E.8, was one of the fifty five [2] submarines of the E class which made up the backbone of Britain's submarine fleet during the First World War. E.8 was one of the first group and was built by the Royal Dockyard at Chatham and launched on 30 October 1913. E.8 had a surface displacement of 655 tons (796 tons submerged) and was 178'1" long with a beam of 22' and mean draught of

12'6". She was powered by two 8-cylinder 1600bhp Vickers diesels giving a speed of 15 knots, but when submerged used two 840hp electric motors powered from batteries which were recharged when the submarine was on the surface. Her armament consisted of four 18" torpedo tubes: one in the bow, two mounted on the beam and one firing astern. Eight torpedoes were carried and she had a complement of thirty officers and men.

The diary begins in August 1915 when Goodhart had been selected to take E.8 into the Baltic to join E.1 (Commander Noel Laurence RN) and E.9 (Commander Max Horton) which were already operating there. The idea of sending British submarines to the Baltic arose almost by accident at a planning conference on 17 September 1914 onboard HMS *Iron Duke*, flagship of the Grand Fleet. Present were: Admiral Sir John Jellicoe, Commander in Chief; Winston Churchill, First Lord of the Admiralty; Vice-Admiral Sir Doveton Sturdee, Jellicoe's chief of staff; Commodore Roger Keyes and Commodore Reginald Tyrwhitt, the commanders of the submarine and destroyer forces at Harwich.

The discussion turned on how best to operate offensively against a seemingly inactive German High Seas Fleet. Churchill proposed sending a substantial force through the Skagerrak and Kattegat into the Baltic to attack the High Seas Fleet at their moorings in Kiel Bay followed by a landing of troops on the Pomeranian coast. It was a 'typically impetuous Churchillian proposal in an increasingly stagnant atmosphere'[3]. Commodore Keyes suggested the more practical alternative of sending submarines into the Baltic. A small number of submarines could wreak havoc on units of the High Seas Fleet which exercised in the safe waters of the Baltic and could also interdict the valuable iron ore trade between Sweden and Germany. There would be danger in entering the Baltic, particularly during the passage of the Sound, the stretch of water between Denmark and Sweden, but Keyes was sure that the risks involved were acceptable. However, Keyes did not foresee that once in the Baltic the boats would be unable to leave once the enemy was alerted, nor did he consider how the boats were to be supplied and maintained. It was entirely typical of Keyes to concentrate on the initial objective of getting the submarines into the Baltic and leave the less interesting details of logistics to be settled later.

Consequently, the crews of the first two submarines, E.1 and E.9, were not properly briefed before attempting the voyage and although both vessels arrived, they had eventful passages. Moreover, the Russians, who had not been consulted about the project, were unsure how best to employ the submarines.

Nevertheless the success of the operations conducted by Laurence and Horton caused a further four British submarines to be ordered there. Goodhart's E.8 and Lieutenant Commander Geoffrey Layton's E.13 were sent in August 1915 followed by another two boats, E.18 and E.19, in September.

Goodhart's diary begins with the preparations for the operation:

> [Sunday 15 August 1915] Yesterday went into town in afternoon with Captain W [4] and Windy Layton [5]. Saw C.O.S VA Oliver [6] and 1st Sea Lord Jackson [7] they were both very nice and wished us all good luck. Got sailing orders from C.O.S also charts. Went with Layton to Carlton and Piccadilly Grill returning by 5.40 train. In morning Isa [8] and Mother came to church. I had a lot to do getting things fixed up with Layton. It is a good job and I do hope we all have luck. Lunch at hotel. Then afterwards in sitting room with Isa, Mother and Ross. Said good-bye to them (the worst part) and they went back by taxi, there having been a bad thunderstorm. Saw Captain W and he gave us all his good wishes. I think it has been kept pretty dark all round really. We shoved off at 6.0 and did a trim [dive] off Rough Buoy. Then off via Hinder. Crew told where we were going!!

Goodhart had been instructed to avoid all contact with shipping, neutral or otherwise, to avoid being reported to the German patrols in the Kattegat and to the south of the Sound. He and Layton had hoped to keep together but by 17 August both boats were having to dive so frequently to avoid shipping that they lost touch with one another.

> [Monday 16 August 1915] A fine clear day. Got sights in forenoon but it clouded over later on. Had to alter course away from a few things notably a steamer steering north for Hautskola in afternoon. Passed rather close to a fishery boat about 6pm. Turned out she was a Swede rather unfortunate but trust she will not be back in port in time to report us. Well up to time and engine going splendidly. Feeling somehow very confident thank God. Expect to have plenty of diving tomorrow.

Goodhart's passage of the Sound was not

without incident. Keeping close to the Swedish side of the channel and running with only the submarine's tiny conning tower above the water, E.8 was spotted by a trawler on 19 August :

> ...he spotted us I think because of searchlights on the Danish shore against which I was shewn up. I was going on one engine, trimmed well down and keeping her up with the planes. He burnt two flares, (and I thought him to be a small trawler or T.B) also altered course for me, we fell down inside and went to the bottom with a dash, as we filled everything (a mistake). Went ahead along bottom (14' on gauge) till we got into slightly deeper water 17-18' ...Then rose to the surface and I put my head out, heading out S 20° W. We were now about 400 yards south of light vessel. The searchlight ship shewing three lights right ahead. Trawler some way off to port making a morse signal. I went ahead and twisted round the ship ahead leaving her to starboard. Then resumed course for deep water. Suddenly sighted a lump ahead which switched on searchlights so down with a rush. Hit bottom an awful crash at 16' (but 23' on gauge) then into 18' but on a ledge on the starboard side. Starboard propeller taken off. Heard propellers aft and up port side about 4 lots. Remained on bottom for a few minutes, no use going ahead on bottom again for fear of losing other propeller. Then came up to surface again, to find destroyer on starboard beam close about 50 to 100 yards off burning single white light at masthead. Dived boat slowly to 14' then 16' then 18' and kept her there. Thank God!

Goodhart found the experience of being harried profoundly unsettling:

> Felt very miserable and could not sleep though very weary. The whole success of the job depended on my being unseen and I felt I had rather let E.13 down by being sighted. At one time had desperate ideas of internment owing to loss of propeller.

Although by this time Goodhart had passed through the Sound and entered the Baltic, his troubles were not yet over for he was spotted by a Swedish train ferry which turned back on sighting the submarine. Though flying Swedish colours the steamer evidently reported the submarine, for a little while later a German destroyer appeared and once again E.8 was harassed by the Germans:

> I went to bottom in 23 fathoms for a rest till dark. Its hard to describe one's feelings but I was very depressed as I have said above. I thought that the steamer was possibly laying nets or mines. Propellers were heard at 2.45 and 5.00 At 6.40 came up for a look and found steamer still there ahead. Dived east till 8.25 when I came to the surface for a look found it moon light and steamer fairly close astern so dived again till 9.30 pm.

The submarine's battery was now very nearly exhausted so Goodhart slowly left the area charging the battery all the time until 01.30 on 20 August. It was then beginning to get light and Goodhart felt that the enemy would surely look for him off Bornholm having been alerted during the night. Goodhart intended to pass well north of Bornholm before altering course for Dagerort where he would be met by a Russian escort. Once passed Bornholm the going was easier but on the morning of the 21 August there was another encounter with the enemy:

> We passed about 16 miles off Gotland and at 1.20pm Greig 9 on watch reported a large black object coming across our bows from westward – dived and when at 40' heard propellers overhead.

Eventually E.18. rendezvoused with a Russian destroyer and the British submarine E.9 of Dagerort on 22 August. There Goodhart heard the news that the crew of E.13 had been interned by the Danes after going ashore on Saltholme Island. Before the Danes could take the crew off, E.13 had been fired on by German destroyers and thirteen of her ship's company killed:

> A Dirty Trick. My opinion is that seeing the flares and searchlights when I was seen she altered course too far to the north ... I do feel very sorry about it, and it makes one's own success in getting out alive rather a qualified one.

For the final stage of the voyage to Reval 10, a Russian naval officer came onboard to assist with pilotage.

Goodhart described him as: 'Quite a good sort, but I didn't care for his scent and he was rather fastidious however we got along all right together ... I had a most interesting yarn with the Russky officer about their fleet.'

E.8 arrived at Reval on the evening 23 August and was docked the next day to have the propeller replaced on her starboard shaft. Goodhart was able to discuss operations with Russian officers and with British submariners who had preceded him and perform the usual round of courtesy calls on Russian naval and military commanders.

> [29 August 1915] The Russians are fine fellows and are wonderfully optimistic. Their navy is doing fine work too, and I believe that their mining knocks that of the Germans into cocked hat.

E.8's first patrol off the Gulf of Riga was from 30 August to 6 September l915 and was a miserable affair dogged by bad weather and with no sightings of the enemy. For his next patrol Goodhart fervently hoped that he would see some action:

> [9 September 1915] I hope I hit something with the fish – it seems we are bound to sight the enemy sometime so hope for good luck ... rotten waiting about like this.

E.8 sailed on the 12 September for a position off Steinort. His first encounter with the enemy was not successful. Faulty torpedo tube drill lost him an opportunity of sinking a U-boat:

> [14 September 1915] About 2.30 sighted a submarine right ahead. I closed her gently & found that she was charging & going very slowly. Small German boat turtle back shape. I approached on opposite course & got too close. On giving order stand by port beam [tube], sluice door not open and we missed the shot. She saw us when abeam and dived. I went SE after her for half an hour and then turned north not seeing her again till this was written 5.15. Rather a nuisance as it looks as if they knew our billets & were waiting for us. Tube not being ready entirely my fault ... She saw me as I was having a good look to make sure she was not Russian & foolishly got Dentre [11] to give his opinion on her.

The following day Goodhart tried to close and attack a cruiser which he identified as one of the Graudenz class (the ship was, in fact, the *Augsberg*) but he could get no closer than five miles. E.8 returned to Reval on 20 September and Goodhart found he had been awarded the order of St. Vladimir for his successful passage of the Sound and entry to the Baltic. This was not the only cause for celebration for Goodhart had managed to secure the promotion of his engineer, Chief Engine Room Artificer John Asker [12].

Following the usual post-patrol repairs, E.8 was out again on 28 September for a coast patrol between Danzig and Bornholm. 1 October was a busy day for after sighting two destroyers and nearly running into a minefield Goodhart:

> ...made out 4 ships, three with one funnel and two masts and the second ship with two fore and aft funnels and two masts. I thought she was one of Hawke type of cruiser and so decided to fire at her. At last moment made usual balls of it! Found I was not close enough for No.2 & had not put the periscope up at the right moment ... went on to fire at third one and missed her somehow. I didn't look where the fish went and feel an awful idiot. They saw the periscope and fired which was pretty smart as they could not have seen me till firing & they then calmly steamed away on their course.

The ships Goodhart had attacked were the auxiliary minelayers *Odin*, *Hugen*, *Hertha* and *Kaiser* which were on their way to lay mines in the Gulf of Riga. Goodhart's morale was obviously at a low ebb:

> [Monday 4 October 1915] Rather sick of this sort of thing and a bit down hearted as I don't seem able to straffe the Germans much.

Finally Goodhart was able to claim his first success:

> [Tuesday 5 October 1915] At 12.08 Smith [13] came along and told me that a large steamer was closing up astern. So closed her a bit. Having decided that she had not got a gun!! I came up on her starboard beam at 12.20. Great flap as International Signal Book was missing. However made signal to stop engines and steamed after her on surface. She took no notice so having got gun ready, I fired a shot

across her bows. (This narrowly missed a lookout on her fxle. [14]) This stopped him and I closed him passing under his stern, I hailed him to abandon ship but he couldn't hear owing to escaping steam. However Miller [15] hailed them in German and they understood and got into their two boats. I didn't board her as we were within 2' (miles) of the lighthouse, and bound to be reported soon, so feared interruption. Her name was Margarette of Konigsberg and flying German merchant flag. When boats had got clear I started firing. She sank bow first to port ... her stern stuck up with the flag flying till about 2.30 when she disappeared altogether.

E.8 returned to Reval to find that everyone was 'bucked up' over Goodhart's sinking. Goodhart had expected some time in harbour but on 17 October was warned to be ready for patrol in place of E.9 since Horton was sick, and in fact sailed the next day for a patrol off Libau. At first this patrol seemed like any other. Trafalgar Day was celebrated with one glass of whiskey and soda – the crew had vodka [16] – and with Goodhart complaining: '...wish we could celebrate it by sinking a dreadnought but fear there is nothing to bring them out.'

Goodhart finally got his wish at 0850 on 23 October:

Pavloff [17] looking out reported smoke on the starboard quarter so I went to look at it and there was plenty of it, so I watched and found its bearing was drawing forward. So went on both motors and steered 340°, then 350°. Fine sunny and nice breeze from SSE a splendid day for an attack from our point of view. By degrees we saw it was a 3 funnel ship 2 very tall masts with tops. Two destroyers were with her doing zig zags on either bow (one each side). I remarked to Greig that they need not worry us, as there were only 2 and the chances enormously against us fouling them! ...I eased down as we closed but it was a really simple attack, I never altered course a degree till well - after firing! Fired bow tube. It is hard to say what really happened. I wasn't (for a wonder) a bit worried till after firing. One destroyer crossed our bow about 200 yards off and I left our periscope up rather a long time (half a minute I expect) just as she was coming on to fire. But torpedo HIT after 75

seconds- just under 1600 yards. I followed the track of the torpedo when I fired and saw it was running well. We came up to c~ 18' on firing so I lowered the periscope a bit. then up again to have a look again. Ship struck me as being a bit small but later think she was either Prinz Adalbert or Pommern class. I was looking right ahead when I suddenly saw a red line of flame along her waterline under the forebridge. I thought they had fired fore turret at me!! & gave the order Port 20° and 50' at once. I looked at the ship and all there was, was an immense cloud of thick smoke, she must have gone off in one act!! A Mark VIII is some stuff, but it must have got her forward magazine. A marvellous sight and terrifically impressive, bits of the ship were splashing in the water fully 500 yards astern of her. The crew were very bucked and clapped.

Elation at his success was followed by the more practical business of clearing the area so that the commanders of the two destroyers who were rescuing survivors should think that a mine was responsible and not a submarine. Once clear, however, there was time for a celebratory bottle of 'fizz' and some reflection:

It's awful to think of the loss of life, but looking at it from the proper war point of view, it's a good bit of work, & everybody onboard deserves it at last.

E.8 returned to Reval on 24 October to a rousing reception:

They gave us a great reception the Dvina (Russians) giving their Russian cheers with the commander prominent on the gangway, then E.9 and E.19 alongside the *Reinda* gave us four good English ones.

Goodhart later learned that the ship he had torpedoed was the German cruiser Prinz Adalbert launched in 1901 and completed in January 1904. He was later presented with a lifebuoy from the cruiser which Laurence's E.1 found in the sea on her next patrol.

Goodhart did one more patrol in November during which he attacked a merchant ship on 7th: the torpedo hit but did not explode. Events at sea were now being overshadowed by a worsening of relations between Horton and Laurence, the two senior British submariners in the Baltic. The origins of the quarrel are impossible to identify and there is nothing on the matter in the official record, although one suggestion is that Horton made some ill-judged comments to Laurence about how he should run his submarine. Both men were highly competent submariners but very different personalities. Laurence, marginally the senior, was austere and remote. Horton was a *bon viveur* with an eye for the ladies and an immense capacity for drink and gambling which endeared him to the Russians. Both men were popular with their subordinates but found it difficult to relate to their contemporaries and superiors. In the confined society of the British community in the Baltic two such powerful personalities could hardly be expected to get on. The situation was exacerbated by there being no senior officer who could keep the two in hand. Goodhart evidently sympathised with Horton:

> [29 October] The one and only solution of the business appears to me to be the appointment of an officer in charge of the Garage senior to Laurence. The latter has not tact and does very rotten things sometimes.

Relations with the Russians were also strained, professional jealousy being the cause since the Russian submariners had failed to match the successes scored by their British allies. Goodhart's opinion of his Russian colleagues had evidently changed in the four months he had spent at Reval:

> [9 November] Their submariners are a rotten lot of officers, it was regarded as their 'bum' job before the war consequently they are not of the best … there is a good feeling of jealousy of the British submariners evident at present.

However, such disagreeable matters were forgotten on 10 November when Tsar Nicholas II visited the submarines to distribute decorations:

> [Wednesday 10 November 1915] A Red Letter Day. Shortly after 8.0 moved boat up alongside *Europa* with E.19. Boats all there preparatory to Tsar's visit in the afternoon. Freezing hard after a little more snow but very cold. E.19 is still a sight her gun all covered up with ice. We didn't get so much coming back but have a certain amount of it, & the sides all ice covered. How our men work their

lines in such weather I don't know. Laurence gave us detail for afternoon performance with Emperor. We all mustered in *Europa* at 12.45. No overcoats as they were hardly respectable! Men in No 3s too & bitterly cold. I had to chose five men to have St. George's Crosses given to them by Emperor. Chose Asker, Perry, Thomas, Maunders, Vale as five best men only doubt being the latter but his tube fired the winning shot …we retired to the wardroom after C-in-C's arrival & made a hurried exit when we heard the Tsar was arriving. Fell-in in our places. The Tsar inspected troops ashore first, who meanwhile made continuing cheering noise & then came onboard followed by a very numerous staff. The Tsar started forward & walked aft shaking hands with us all, & saying something to everybody He talks excellent English and is a much finer looking (though very like) man than our King...He said how elated they all were when they heard of the P.A's defeat & I said we in the boat were enormously elated too! He then gave Cromie [18] and I St George's Cross saying he had much pleasure in presenting us with them. All I could think of to say was 'Thank you'. The young Tsarevitch was with him, a lively looking young boy in grey overcoat & St George's medal cross… and I had to get over the other side of the deck to be present when medals were given to our men. I gave the names of each man in turn and he gave the crosses, thanking each man personally for what he had done. The men were awfully bucked up over it all.

The day was not yet over for Goodhart had to show two senior Russian officers over his submarine [where one fell down the after periscope well and had to be extricated] before he was invited to dine aboard the Imperial train with Cromie, Laurence and Horton, 'A more palatial railway carriage I have never seen.'

The grand events of the 10th were totally eclipsed the next day with the news that E.8 had been badly damaged in a collision with the Russian submarine *Gepard*:

> Went over to the dock with Simpson and found that *Gepard* had left her hydroplanes stuck into anchor weight casting. It penetrated into No.2 compartment! No.1

Commander Francis Goodhart (right) photographed in 1916 with his first lieutenant, Lieutenant Alexander Greig. Goodhart Collection HU 57575.

British submarine officers onboard the depot ship *Dvina* at Reval in 1916. Front row (left to right): Commander F H Goodhart, commanding officer E.8; Commander F N A Cromie, commanding officer E.9; Lieutenant Commander Hubert Vaughan-Jones, commanding officer E.9. Rear row (left to right) Sub-Lieutenant E F St.John; Lieutenant J J R Peirson, navigating officer E.9; Lieutenant A Fenner, commanding officer E.1; Lieutenant A Bertram Smith RNR; Lieutenant Miller, Russian liaison officer and Lieutenant von Essen, Russian liaison officer. Goodhart collection HU 57591.

E.8 returning from patrol in the summer of 1916. Goodhart Collection HU 57612.

Russian cavalry on the Galician front. These men are from the regiment reviewed by Goodhart and the other British submariners on 9 March 1916. Goodhart Collection HU 57593.

Officers on the bridge of E.9 in the Baltic.From left to right: Engineer-Lieutenant Cecil Simpson; Commander Max Horton, commanding officer; Lieutenant von Essen, Russian liaison officer and Lieutenant Charles Chapman, first lieutenant. Goodhart Collection HU 57608

external flank) got two holes made by her propeller blades. At least a six weeks job I'm afraid. Forward firing tube finished anyway …very downhearted at the job.

Though he was exonerated by a Court of Enquiry, Goodhart was immensely depressed at the prospect of a long period of inactivity.

His bleak mood was not improved by the prospect of all the British submarines moving to

Helsingfors and ceasing operations for the winter. The idea was Laurence's and supported by the Russians. Goodhart was unenthusiastic and suspected Laurence of having ulterior motives:

[18 November] I cannot see any reason in laying boats up longer than necessary when those boats may be the only active force working against the enemy. Of course, Laurence wants Helsingfors but I don't mind saying here that it would be far better if L were not here. He does not look beyond his own comfort and interests and is not over keen on going to sea at any time. The idea of our being shut up like that perhaps needlessly, when there is so much to be done is awful & what will it look like when history is written?

Goodhart's comments are a little too harsh since Laurence finished the war as one of the most highly decorated submarine commanders, a DS0 and bar, and the only submariner - ever- to hit two battleships with the same salvo [19] but his comments reflect the bitterness and despair he felt at being inactive.

Since E.8 was in dockyard hands, Goodhart was able to pay a visit to Petrograd where apart from professional discussions at the Russian Admiralty he was cheered at the opera:

[26 November] A dreadful moment arose

Officers on the bridge of HM Submarine E.18 shortly before she was lost in the summer of 1916. From left to right: Sub-Lieutenant Douglas Colson DSC RNR, navigating officer; Lieutenant Commander R C Halahan, commanding officer; Lieutenant Walter Landale, first lieutenant. Goodhart Collection HU 57589.

Officers on the bridge of HM Submarine E.8 on her return to Reval on 2 November 1916. Goodhart is the centre figure on the conning tower. Goodhart Collection HU 57611.

British and Russian officers during their visit to the Crimea and Galician front in 1916. From left to right: Russian railway official; Russian steward; Commander F N A Cromie; Lieutenant A Fenner; Sub-Lieutenant E F St.John; Lieutenant A Bertram Smith RNR; Lieutenant von Essen; Lieutenant Commander Vaughan-Jones and Commander F H Goodhart. Goodhart collection HU 57597.

between the 3rd and 4th acts we were taken round the house by Igoravuitch [20] and back to box rather early (a put-up job). They then played national anthems, Rule Britannia for ours and clapped us like anything. Did not know what to do or where to look but managed a salute somehow and a sort of bow. Very embarrassing! but one felt it was a good show somehow as it would buck them all up. Shall have to do something more to deserve it all.

On his return to Reval, Goodhart found that E.8 was still in dockyard hands and that as a result he would miss participating in a forthcoming operation. His despondent mood was not improved on 6 December when Horton told him that he was going back to England and he took the unprecedented step of complaining directly to Admiral Phillimore: [21]

> [6 December] Laurence has made a hopeless mess of things here. Decided in afternoon to write a letter to Admiral Phillimore on subject & jeopardise my own career by criticising my superior service officer. Horton has received a message to say that his relief will be sent out & that really is the limit! I can't stick it under L. He is such a wicked fool. It is obviously one's duty to put a word in on the matter now.

In the event the complaint proved unnecessary since Laurence's behaviour had already aroused Phillimore's concern and as a result Phillimore visited Reval on 15 December and saw the officers individually. Goodhart also learned that Laurence was being relieved.

There was no progress with the work of repairing E.8 which had now developed problems with her battery necessitating the removal of one of the cells. Goodhart had hoped to have E.8 ready for trials after Christmas but the problems with the battery were more serious than first thought and the whole battery now had to be lifted out of the boat. To complicate matters, the battery repair and charging facilities of the dockyard at Reval were extremely primitive and could only handle a quarter of E.8's battery at a time. It was going to be an 'awful job' and would delay E.8's return to sea for some time.

1916 began with Goodhart in a '...very sad state for me owing to last night's orgy having bad effects in the morning.' The alcoholic celebrations were not yet over for, on 2 January, Goodhart found he was promoted commander in the New Year promotion list and on the same day Horton departed for England, – the cause for further celebrations:

> ...a fine lunch with much wine. Horton made fine speeches and so did others. Said something myself too but don't remember

what it was! Returned onboard about 4.00 with Commander Cokhill [22] & told him about everything which was rather unwise perhaps. Then wrote to Isa a bit more, but I wonder what on earth she will think of my!! condition. Had a little dinner and then drove with Horton & Essen [23] in car to station. – A wonderfully good send off to old Horton and his crew turned up & there was a terrific din...fear I was rather bottled.

Laurence followed Horton back to England on 9 January but:

> [8 January] He has asked especially that there shall be no 'drunken' speeches or drunken brawl at the railway station.

> [9 January] We made no speeches as per request of yesterday, I didn't feel like it after such an insulting reference to Horton's departure! He went off to station after that & departed. I did not see him off for similar reasons.

E.8 was still in dockyard hands having her battery lifted and repaired and there was little for Goodhart to do other than routine duties, writing letters (he was a frequent and diligent correspondent to his wife), Russian lessons and conversation with fellow officers. It would be some time before the battery was ready, so on 14 February Goodhart was among a party of British submariners who departed for Petrograd by train to visit Moscow before beginning a tour of the Caucasus and the Galician front.

> [19 February] We have had a good time in Moscow & of course it is all absolutely unique for me & us all. One gets curious insights into political life here but I think after the war the change must take place to a really representative government.

> [21 February] ..we were passing through a country rather like our Downs but browner. It continued like that till we reached Sebastopol...the place is rather like Malta on a grand scale.

> [22 February] we all went onboard submarine depot. The lunch..developed into the

customary drinking business and we had short sharp speeches and a huge flagon full of fizz for the English officers!

From Sebastopol the party proceeded to the southern sector of the Galician front:

[3 March] We got to Kumeneats Podolski about 9.30pm having spent a rotten time in the carriage singing &. Found some officers who met us and took us to hotels Belle Vue and Bristol. Cromie, Fenner, I and Malzoff [24] went to the former. A poor place, round house filthy and no bath. However we don't expect luxuries here.

[5 March] Resumed our journey to Germachoufka..on arrival we drove to the headquarters of 41st Army Corps. After lunch we got into fresh sleighs to go to Skuparkathi 1st Platoon Brigade Cossack Headquarters. I felt absolutely sea-sick from the motion, we went faster and the snow was in ridges like waves so what with lumbago, swollen tonsils and head I did not feel up to much on arrival. We are now about eight versts [25] from the actual front and this village is sometimes shelled. We settled down in the mess of the officers- all Cossacks and very fine fellows. I had meant to go to bed for an hour or so to get rid of head but we waited for the general. He did not get back till 9.45 after we had had dinner. He made speeches in Russian welcoming us and was a very cheerful bird... he gave us a Cossack dance & song & so did others General finally doing one & firing revolvers off twice into the ceiling during it.

[6 March] We drove to where the troops in reserve are kept in dug-outs or bomb proof shelters, very cosy and warm. There were a number of men drilling for sergeants & general got them all up & told them who were & all cheered &c, &c & we had quite a review. When we reached the front line the general introduced us to the men there and they cheered. The men in trenches quite clean & had been there 45 days! & quite happy. Austrians never attack nowadays and seem to have got their tails down. Very good men here look wild but awfully fit. The enemy seemed to spot our movements somehow , as rifle fire was kept up all along as we went away & you could hear the ping of the bullets. An officer gave me a bullet which had just arrived in the back wall of the trench just missing his head. it was pretty nervy work & I could not help ducking lots of times. I'm afraid I should never do in the trenches as I'm much too great a coward.

[9 March] Feeling rotten. Field horse Artillery and another cavalry regiment all did drills. I was so bored and cold that I did not pay much attention to it.

[15 March] Arrived at Dear Old Reval about 8.50.

Goodhart found his submarine in much the same condition as he had left her as the battery had not been fully repaired. It would not be until 9 May that the work was finished and so for two months Goodhart simply had to wait. Even then E.8 was not operational for the bow torpedo tube was out of alignment and there were a number of other irritating equipment failures which all combined to keep E.8 in the dockyard. Finally on 25 May, over six months after her collision with *Gepard*, E.8 went on patrol off Libau. The patrol was uneventful and she returned to Reval on 31May. E.8 was once again under repair, this time for the re-alignment of a propeller shaft. Goodhart was not pleased:

[5 June] Fine hot day. Went in yard. Very little doing. Heard later that shaft was spoiled by dockyard workmen in night, means a delay of four days. Awful rot and I am sending an official report on the matter.

Goodhart was also worried about the fate of E.18, commanded by Lieutenant Commander R C Halahan, which had gone on patrol on 24 May with E.8 but which had not returned:

[5 June] All very worried about E.18, each day makes her absence more serious and I fear there is no hope of her return now.

[6 June] Am afraid E.18 has gone as no news whatever.

[7 June] Heard from Essen that their W.T had vaguely indicated presence of a submarine off Redshoff on Monday. Very slender hope but some hope still.

[8 June] Had a confab during which E.18 question talked of. Cromie said she had fifteen days food. Very hopeless now I fear. No news whatever [26].

E.8's various defects kept her in harbour so Goodhart occupied himself with routine duties and tennis with the British consul, Mr William Girard, and his family. Finally, on 20 July E.8 was ready for sea.

Goodhart's time was now spent in increasing efforts to keep E.8 operational- her growing list of defects was inevitable given that the submarine had gone for well over a year without a major refit. Despite having to spend such a large time in harbour Goodhart's diary contains few references to conditions in Russia or the growing instability of the government or the scandals affecting the Imperial family. Goodhart, and indeed the rest of the British submariners, lived in a self-contained society made up of themselves, the small expatriate British community ashore and such Russian officers as they came into contact with.

On 2 November, Goodhart learned that E.8 would be given a comprehensive refit at Reval. Goodhart's last patrol in the submarine was from 27 October to 2 November. The area was the familiar billet off Libau and the patrol was uneventful except for bad weather.

[15 December] A dull wet day. In yard all forenoon arranging about defect list and new wardroom. Mail in afternoon...went into Cromie's cabin and found there my appointment to DOLPHIN!!!!!!!! [27] Mad with joy.

[25 December] Girard spoke and brought out our leaving which resulted in 'For he's a Jolly Good Fellow' etc. & cheers most embarrassing. Said a few words but awfully mixed....am quite sorry now to be leaving but not for 'home' reasons.

[26 December] There will be a big stunt at the station tonight. Went to the station in a car. It was a wonderful experience there. Had some trouble in finding the right carriage but got to it eventually. The sailors put us up on their shoulders repeatedly. Everybody was there, C-in-C's band and the C-in-C himself but he could not get on the platform! One felt one could hardly realise the business at all really..all the crew were there, an enormous stunt.

Goodhart returned home via Sweden to Bergen in Norway and thence by ship to Newcastle where he arrived on 4 January 1917:

[4 January 1917] I got up about 7.0. We were in harbour up the Tyne close to the high level bridge. Got breakfast and got ashore first at 9.0am. Military police very good getting our gear through etc. Sent off wires to Isa at Regents Palace and Budleigh. It was ripping being in England again & a bright sunny day. We 'got luncheon baskets and tea and arrived at Kings X at 5.15. I put my heavy gear in the cloakroom and went by taxi to the Regents Palace Hotel. Got a wire there from Isa to say that she would reach Waterloo 5.10. No rooms but they referred me to Loudon Hotel Surrey St. so went there and got a room. Then to Foreign Office and delivered bags and got my own papers. Then to Regents Palace and found Isa just arriving so took her on to Loudon hotel. Jolly good to see her again.

[Friday 5 January 1917] I am go to Greenock [28] for K.14 [29]. They seem great boats.

[Monday 8 January 1917] Got to Glasgow (St Enochs) at 9.15 and got breakfast in hotel. After lunch went to Fairfields by train having a few miseries on the way. Found Herbert [30] and he shewed me round his boat K.13. Very terrifying to look at and full of workmen. He says they are an awful crowd here, awful trade unionism etc. Rather fed up at having to build here. Very lonely in hotel.

[Tuesday 9 January 1917] I went around to the works and went around with Herbert and saw my boat on the slips (which will be launched about the end of the month). In afternoon went over K.14 with Mr Weaver, a sort of super-foreman.

From 9 January until 24th Goodhart was on leave at the family home at Budleigh Salterton in Devon. The diary entries for this period reflect his pleasure at being back in England and being able to spend time with his family, especially his new daughter, Barbara, whom he had not seen.

Goodhart brought his wife up to Greenock to be with him while K.14 was completed and the couple took rooms in the same house as Commander Herbert and his wife. On 29 January, Goodhart accepted an invitation to come out with him in K.13 which was going to make her first dive in the Gareloch. It was the usual practice for the commanding officers of submarines under construction to accompany another of the same class on her trials so that they could gain experience of the submarine's handling characteristics.

All went well during the trials despite some trouble with the boiler room fans and a final dive was to be made after lunch before Herbert formally accepted K.13 from the builders. During this dive the boiler room flooded and K.13, unable to surface, sank stern first to the bottom of the Gareloch.

Goodhart volunteered to make a daring escape from the submarine, carrying details of the submarine's condition and a list of surviving members of the crew. The plan was for Goodhart and Herbert to enter the submarine's conning tower and close the lower hatch, thereby sealing themselves off from the rest of the submarine. The two men would then flood the conning tower until the pressure equalised with that of the sea outside. Goodhart would then open the upper hatch and groping his way through the chart-room overhead, find the exit hatch and head for the surface. Once Goodhart was clear, Herbert would secure the hatch and, by knocking on the deck, signal to those in the control room that they could drain down the conning tower. However the plan went awry, as Herbert recalled:

I remember Goodhart knocking off the upper hatch clips and saying he was ready. Then he ducked under the water level and was followed through the hatch by a tremendous rush of air. Thinking he was safely away I took a breath of air...ducked under water also, and tried to bring down the hatch and clip it. But here Providence took the matter in care so that, without any option on my part, I was carried through the hatch and into the chart room. Somehow I managed to find the small loose flap, and go through...and came to the surface in a tremendous surge of air, close alongside a boat with a ladder on which was standing a diver without his helmet. As he grabbed me and began helping me into the boat, my first words 'Where's Goodhart?' were answered by a shake of the head. Nothing had been seen of him. [31]

Goodhart had, in fact, shot out of the conning tower at such speed that he had hit his head on the roof of the wheelhouse, been rendered unconscious and subsequently drowned. For his final act of bravery Goodhart was posthumously awarded the Albert Medal.

The Goodhart diaries [32] constitute a detailed record of one of the little known aspects of the war at sea in the First World War. They give an excellent picture of the early days of submarine warfare and show the enthusiasm of the early submariners for their craft with no hint of the unbelievably squalid conditions in which they lived while at sea. The diaries are also an excellent evocation of the late Edwardian period and with their talk of 'bucking up', 'good shows' and 'straffing', they recall the naivety with which the generation of 1914 approached the age of total war.

The last entry in the diary is written by Goodhart's wife, Isabel.

[Monday 29 January] Frank left at 6 a.m to go with Mr Herbert in K.13. He never came back. The boat sank at 3. p.m off Shandon and on Tuesday the 30 at 1 p.m Frank was drowned trying to get out of the boat to get help - His body was found on Feb. 1st and on the 6th he was buried at Faslane Cemetery – Garelochhead.

Notes

1. Although Goodhart refers to Fairfields' yard as being at Greenock, in fact the shipyard was located at Govan. Perhaps he was confusing Fairfields' with that other well-known builder of submarines, Scotts, whose yard was located at Greenock.

2. Fifty seven if the Australian AE.1 and AE.2 are included.

3. Richard Compton-Hall, *Submarines and the War at Sea 1914-1918*, Macmillan, London, 1991, p.135.

4. Captain Arthur Waistell, Captain (S) 8th Submarine Flotilla at Harwich.

5. Lieutenant Commander Geoffrey Layton, commanding officer of HMS/M E.13, nick-named 'Windy' on account of his non-stop chatter.

6. Vice-Admiral Sir Henry Oliver, Chief of the Naval Staff.

7. Admiral Sir Henry Jackson, First Sea Lord.

8. Isabel Goodhart, his wife to whom he wrote frequently while in the Baltic.

9. Lieutenant Alexander Greig RN, E.8's first lieutenant.

10. Now Tallinn in Estonia.

11. Russian naval officer appointed to E.8 for liaison duties.

12. During the First World War it was rare for a submarine to carry a commissioned officer as an engineer.

13. Lieutenant A B Smith RNR, navigating officer of E.8.

14. Fxle - an abbreviation for forecastle, the forward part of the ship.

15. Lieutenant Boris Miller: Russian liaison officer appointed to E.8. Miller was usually appointed to E.1 but sailed with E.8 on this patrol as Goodhart was dissatisfied with Dentre.

16. The rum beloved of the British sailor had run out and no further supplies were available.

17. Lieutenant I Pavloff, the Russian liaison officer who had replaced Dentre.

18. Lt Cdr F N A Cromie RN, commanding officer of HM Submarine E.19. After Laurence's departure, Cromie became the senior British submariner in north Russia and following the Bolshevik Revolution became British Naval Attaché in Petrograd. He was murdered on 31 August 1918 by a mob which had invaded the embassy.

19. On 5 November 1916 Laurence, in command of J.1, torpedoed *Kronprinz* and *Grosser Kurfurst* with the same salvo.

20. Commander V I Igoravuitch:

submarine liaison officer at the Russian Admiralty.

21. Admiral R F Phillimore, the British naval representative at Stavka, Russian Supreme Headquarters.

22. Russian engineer officer.

23. Lieutenant Otto von Essen, son of the Commander-in-Chief of the Russian Baltic Fleet, and liaison officer with the British submarine flotilla.

24. The Russian liaison officer escorting the party. Rank and forenames are not given.

25. Russian measure of distance, roughly two thirds of a mile.

26. E.18 was presumed sunk off Bornholm on 24 May 1916 by a German decoy vessel.

27. HMS *Dolphin*, the home of the Royal Navy's Submarine Service at Gosport.

28. See note 1.

29. HMS K.14: a steam driven submarine of the K Class: 1980/2566 tons; 330' x 26' x 17'; ten 18" torpedo tubes, two 4" QF and one 3" QF guns; two shaft Brown-Curtis geared steam turbines; four electric motors; 10,500shp/1440hp, 24/ 9.5 knots; 59 officers and men.

30. Commander Godfrey Herbert, commanding officer of K.13.

31. E Keble Chatteron, *Amazing Adventure*, Hurst and Blackett, London, 1935, p208.

32. Department of Documents, 92/53/1.

Acknowledgements

The author is grateful to Margaret Bidmead, Archivist at the Royal Navy Submarine Museum at Gosport, and to Lieutenant Commander Brian Head RD* RNR for their assistance with this article.

Further Reading

Richard Compton-Hall, *Submarines and the War at Sea 1914-1918*, Macmillan, London, 1991.

E Keble Chatterton, Amazing *Adventure,* Hurst and Blackett London, 1935.

Paul Kemp, *British Submarines of the First World War,* Arms and Armour Press, London, 1990.

Michael Wilson, *Baltic Assignment,* Leo Cooper, London, 1985.

The Whitehall Cenotaph: an accidental monument

Penelope Curtis

Penelope Curtis is Head of the Henry Moore Centre for the Study of Sculpture, Leeds.

On 13 May 1919, Lionel Earle, Permanent Secretary at the Office of Works, wrote to his friend the Earl of Derby, the British Ambassador in Paris, asking him 'to find out without delay the general proposals for the decoration of the Paris streets on the occasion of Peace'. [1] Derby replied that he had been told that there would probably be some sort of movable monument, or catafalque which would form the centre of a procession, an altar at the Pantheon, 25,000 troops, and water displays at a total predicted cost of over 12 million francs. 'This is lavish indeed,' observed Earle. [2]

The British Peace Celebrations Committee had met for the first time a week earlier, with no idea at this stage when the Germans would sign the Treaty of Versailles. Unlike the Prime Minister – who thought that peace celebrations, when they came, should be spontaneous – a body of opinion wished to get preparations under way. At its meeting of 18 June the War Cabinet recorded their 'respectful dissent' from the Prime Minister and agreed that a telegram be dispatched to inform the Dominions that if Peace were signed, the occasion would be marked during Saturday 2 August and the three following days, and that the public should be warned not to indulge in premature celebrations. [3]

The varied proposals for the celebrations recorded at this meeting include no mention of any cenotaph. The only monuments mentioned were Brock's Queen Victoria Memorial at Buckingham Palace – opposite which the King was to take the military salute – and Nelson's Column, both of which were to be decorated. [4]

Peace was signed at the end of June and Lord Curzon hurriedly convened a meeting for 1 July, at which it was decided to bring forward the celebrations to 19 July. Curzon then introduced Lloyd George's suggestion that, following the French example, a catafalque feature in the Victory March, and put the matter into the hands of the First Commissioner of Works, Sir Alfred Mond.

By 8 July Sir Edwin Lutyens's name had appeared in *The Times* as the architect of a 'temporary but fitting monument'. By then Lutyens had produced a number of sketches to meet Lloyd George's demand for a catafalque and had introduced the alternative 'cenotaph'. Mary Lutyens quotes a letter from her father from 7 July in which he reported:

Lord Curzon has approved my structure in Whitehall – but wanted it if possible less catafalqué so I am putting a great vase or basin on it – to spout a pillar of flame at night and I hope smoke by day.

(There is some confusion as to the dating of Lutyens's first involvement in the project; his sketches date to June and July 1919, as do the accounts of his visits to Downing Street.) [5]

Sketch made by Sir Edward Lutyens for the Cenotaph. IWM ART 16377(1). The purchase of this drawing by the Museum was made possible by a grant from the National Art Collections Fund.

Lutyens was already very much involved in the official commemoration of the war. In July 1917 he had gone to France on behalf of the newly established Imperial War Graves Commission and in 1918 had been appointed one of the Principal Architects for the war cemeteries of France and Belgium. He designed the 'War Stone' or gravemarker, and over fifty war memorials in France and Britain during the 1920s. The apparent simplicity of the Cenotaph was to mark the beginning of a style which culminated in the great memorial at Thiepval and which used entasis, curvature and setback, applying mathematical ratios to functional designs.

The *Official Programme of National Peace Celebrations* of 19 July makes no reference to a cenotaph,

but Haig's orders of the same date for the Victory March include, at article 14:

> On reaching the catafalque erected in Whitehall, the left column will keep to the left and the right column to the right. The commands "Eyes right" or "left" will be given when passing the catafalque. Bands marching with the column will not play while passing the catafalque. [6]

There is also an undated memo from the Office of Works on the subject of 'decorations':

> A catafalque to be erected of timber and plaster to the design of Sir Edwin Lutyens in the middle of the road of Whitehall, approximately opposite to the Home Office. [7]

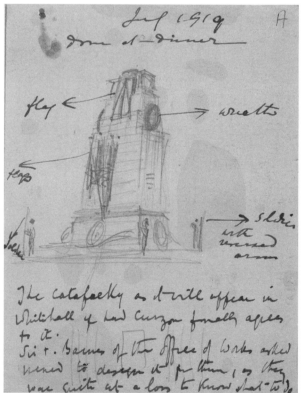

Sketch made by Sir Edward Lutyens for the Cenotaph. IWM ART 16377(3). The purchase of this drawing by the Museum was made possible by a grant from the National Art Collections Fund.

The temporary structure (not, as yet, known as the Cenotaph) by Lutyens was used on the Peace March of 19 July 1919, and was saluted by General Pershing, Marshal

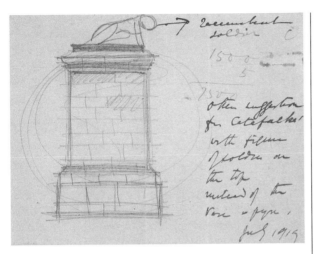

Sketch made by Sir Edward Lutyens for the Cenotaph. IWM ART 16377(4). The purchase of this drawing by the Museum was made possible by a grant from the National Art Collections Fund.

Foch, Field-Marshal Haig [8] and Admiral Beatty. Its architect was not invited to the ceremony. This was not exceptional, for at the unveiling of monuments it was still rare for the artist or architect to be acknowledged alongside those whom they commemorated and those who had commissioned them. It was only as public sculpture lost its commemorative role that the artist came to the fore – the monument coming to signify him rather than the absent. Moreover, this event was not an unveiling as such, for the Cenotaph was more of a stage prop within the ceremony. Ironically, though it was without doubt the Peace March and the illustrious salutes which brought about the realisation of the Cenotaph as a monument, it was the success of its design which made Lutyens's name as an architect. The absence of a real inauguration ceremony for the Cenotaph meant that its ownership was never formally transferred from the initiating body to the collectivity. The terms of ownership were never, and have never been, defined.

The Cenotaph was a temporary monument executed by staff at the Office of Works working round the clock in the five days available to them. An internal memorandum written a few days after the ceremony even gives Sir Frank Baines's staff credit for all the structural details: 'refinements were such that even the separate stones were coloured to give the effect of masonry'. [9]

Three days after the Peace Procession it was decided to allow the Memorial to the Dead in Whitehall to remain in position for another week to allow people travelling to London to see it 'as the outward symbol of the national gratitude'. [10]

But only two days later the Office realised that it would be difficult to remove the cenotaph at the end of the week because of the number of wreaths. [11] That flowers should be laid at the Cenotaph was not in itself unusual; what is notable is how quickly it was adopted as a large-scale version of the street shrine which was found on street corners all over the country.

Lionel Earle felt it was advisable to take prompt action:

> The public would go on placing floral tributes on this monument months hence, and it is rapidly becoming a war shrine. In view of the extremely temporary character of the erection, I think that it should be removed some time… next week… at the same time as the other decorations in connection with the Pageant. [12]

There was no automatic assumption that the Cenotaph should be made permanent, and although such suggestions were made almost as soon as the temporary erection had served its purpose, Bonar Law suggested leaving the decision for about a month. 'In his view, it was too soon after the Peace Procession to judge whether the public opinion, which was now so strongly in favour of the Cenotaph, would continue to be so'. [13]

A significant reason for the Cenotaph's retention, expressed in particular by Mond, was to preclude public controversy over the correct form for a permanent memorial. [14]

As early as 23 July Mond suggested to the War Cabinet that it consider making the memorial a permanent one because of public interest and favourable press opinion. He added that Lutyens himself had expressed 'his readiness to design one on the same lines, with more elaboration'. As points in favour he cited the following:

1. It will be the historic spot.

2. The monument itself is dignified and simple and the position is a central and fine one.

3. The public has become accustomed to seeing the monument on its present site.

4. The erection of a monument on these lines in a permanent form will solve the difficult question of a War Memorial which is bound to become the subject of interest.

As points against, he put forward:

1. Busy thoroughfare.

2. The monument, although appropriate for the occasion, may not be regarded as sufficiently important and may be of too mournful a character as a permanent expression of the triumphant victory of our armies.

3. There will probably be a demand for a greater and more imposing monument in any event.

4. Flowers and wreaths difficult to control – might develop into an unseemly untidiness.

Sketch made by Sir Edward Lutyens for the Centopah. IWM ART 16377(5). The purchase of this drawing by the Museum was made possible by a grant from the National Art Collections Fund.

5. Grounds belong to Westminster Borough Council. [15]

Mond added, 'The proposal to erect a replica of the present design on some other site would seem to me scarcely worthy of consideration. The whole point would be lost.' [16]

The options considered appear to have been either the Cenotaph on the site of the procession, or another monument on another site. There was no question of the Cenotaph going elsewhere. In later years the Office of Works received an enquiry as to whether the site on which the Cenotaph stood had actually been consecrated. This enquiry caused some consternation, for it was soon realised that its consecration had, until then, been simply an assumption. The effective 'consecration' of the Whitehall site by the Victory March was probably as important as Lutyens's design (indeed it was seen to compensate for the modesty of that design) for the erection of the permanent version. The 'sentimental' argument was significant. As the site had been 'consecrated' it was felt it should be permanently protected, and Lutyens was asked to prepare his drawings to allow work to begin in early October, 'so that the site is never again given over for normal traffic'. [17]

The answer to a suggestion in Parliament that the Cenotaph be moved to Parliament Square made it clear that this would be a mistake.

Artistically it would be a blunder. From the point of view of association it would be a crime. [18]

Lutyens felt similarly:

The site has been qualified by the salute of Foch and the allied armies and by our men… [19]

and a journalist summed it up:

It is recognised universally as the right thing in the right place. It is "The Whitehall Cenotaph" and it cannot and must not be anything else. [20]

It was not only the site that was seen as sacred. On 13 November the curator of the Imperial War Museum, Charles ffoulkes, asked Earle if he might have for the museum the sarcophagus which had been on the top of the Cenotaph.

Scene in Whitehall after the Peace Day celebrations of 19 July 1919. Q28762.

All the allied troops in London have saluted this piece of plaster and thousands of men and women have paid reverent respect. [21]

The wood was also saved, and given to a hostel for blinded servicemen where it was made into photo-frames. [22] Such was the sacred aura which now surrounded the Cenotaph that the authorities felt obliged to conceal its absence from the site while the temporary structure was being replaced by the permanent one. [23] The Office of Works specified that 'No demolition will take place or flowers be removed until this scaffold is completed and the Cenotaph hidden from public view'. [24]

On 15 September Earle, prepared for some delay, decided to postpone interfering with the original until the money for the permanent monument was voted. [25] In the event, the temporary Cenotaph was still in Whitehall in December, while Earle waited for the vote to go through Parliament. [26] The temporary structure was beginning to show the effects of the weather, and the Office pushed for a prompt settlement. [27]

As the site was 'sacred', so the public expected decorous behaviour there. In 1924 a member of the

public complained to Ramsay MacDonald that he had been able to see the faded wreaths being piled up in a barrow. [28] The Office of Works gave assurance that, in future, the removal of the wreaths would be completed by 9.00am. [29] The Office frequently had to contend with members of the public shocked and distressed to find that their wreaths had been removed. They frequently interpreted the authorities' action as virtually iconoclastic and appear to have regarded the site of the Cenotaph as inviolate. The Prime Minister must have compounded the authorities' difficulties when, at an early stage, he personally gave the instruction that no wreaths should be removed. [30] As the symbolic stature of the Cenotaph grew and gained meaning for individual members of the public, it became an increasingly difficult site to regulate. A whole framework for the maintenance and regulation (both practical and symbolic) of the Cenotaph had to be instituted (a responsibility which, *faute de mieux*, devolved upon the Office of Works), and this framework frequently clashed with public expectations.

Lutyens had told Mond on 29 July that he would like the monument to be on the same site, and would greatly regret the addition of bronze sentries to the monument, as had been suggested. [31] Mond replied that he had persuaded the Cabinet to approve, and that it should be altered as little as possible. [32] The Cenotaph, if erected at all, had to be erected in the form used for the Peace Procession. It was now seen as unalterable. Neither Lutyens – nor any other architect – would be given the chance to reconsider or improve on it. As a contemporary critic wrote in *Country Life:*

No doubt he could redesign with success. But that is not what is wanted. It would no longer

Crowds outside Buckingham Palace during the Peace Day celebrations, 19 July 1919. Q28765

be the Peace Day Cenotaph, and it is permanence of the Peace Day Cenotaph that is demanded. We want it as we have seen it, merely its plaster transmuted into stone, its emblems into bronze. [33]

Nor could functions or symbolism be altered. Bonar Law explained, in a letter in the *Pall Mall Gazette* to the 'Comrades of the Great War', that 'the Cenotaph is intended to represent an Imperial grave of all those citizens of the Empire' an that it would be unsuitable to convert it into an actual grave. [34]

Finally, on 23 October 1919, the War Cabinet sanctioned a permanent memorial at an approximate cost of £10,000 and decreed that it 'should be a replica exact in every detail – no alterations, additions or fresh inscriptions'. [35] The inscriptions ('The Glorious Dead MCMXIX') were not altered, despite suggestions from a variety of people, including the Archbishop of Canterbury, for 'more suitable' religious or poetic quotations. [36] Lutyens did make slight alterations – 'almost imperceptible, yet sufficient to give it a sculpturesque quality and life, that cannot pertain to rectangular blocks of stone'. These alterations in the curvature were not remarked upon, but Lutyens's proposal to introduce stone flags – 'built in solid with the structure' and impregnated with colour – was greeted with alarm. [37] The Minister of Agriculture and Fisheries alerted his colleagues to this suggestion that the national flags be reproduced in *carved and dyed Portland stone*, and professed that he could not imagine 'anything less calculated to inspire reverence than a petrified and raddled imitation of free and living bunting'. [38] Although Sir Alfred Mond defended the wish of the architect (then absent in India) to have flags in stone rather than 'flimsy textile', and complained that his colleagues' decision, made without any reference to him, made his 'relations with Artists impossible', [39] the Cabinet proceeded to vote for silk flags and textile wreaths. [40]

Later, in 1923, the question arose of placing a light on the Cenotaph, but the press was adamant on this point:

> The simplicity [41] and adequacy of the Cenotaph are very precious.

> Leave the Cenotaph alone. The splendid simplicity was recognised as soon as it was seen. It is finely English'. [42]

The Chancellor of the Exchequer, Austen Chamberlain,

finally bowed to the wishes of the War Cabinet and granted Mond the necessary £10,000 [43], and accordingly, in December 1919, the House of Commons duly voted the money required for the Cenotaph's re-erection. [44]

The work of building the Cenotaph was carried out by Holland and Hannen and Cubitt Ltd, for an estimate of £5,890 submitted in April 1920. Their estimate was the lowest of eight submitted. They contracted to finish work by 23 July 1920. [45] The noted academic sculptor Francis Derwent Wood modelled the wreaths. The present Cenotaph is 35 feet high, with a base measuring 15' x 8'6", and cost £7,325. [46] Lutyens declined any payment:

> as an architect I don't want to be an undertaker and I am too jolly grateful not to be whitening in France myself. [47]

In late September 1920 Earle learned that despite the King's initial reluctance to unveil the Cenotaph, he now accepted that it was the 'general desire on the part of the public'. [48]

During October the format of the inauguration ceremony was under discussion. It was recognised that the order of the day would affect all such ceremonies in the future. Indeed, the 1919 ceremony had already set up something of a formula for an Armistice Day, and the major difference in 1920 was the actual unveiling of the Cenotaph itself. Options discussed included a two minutes' silence (introduced in 1919), playing the 'Last Post', laying a wreath, the hymn 'O God, Our Help in Ages Past', and the delivery prayer by the Archbishop of Canterbury. [49] The Cabinet made a first choice in October, [50] which was subsequently affected by the decision to bring together the unveiling of the Cenotaph and the burying of the unknown 'British Warrior' in Westminster Abbey. [51] On 2 November the Cabinet Memorial Services Committee decided that the service should begin with a hymn, followed by the Lord's Prayer, the unveiling, two minutes' silence, and the 'Last Post'. They would recommend 'simultaneous observance' throughout the Empire. 15,000 applications for tickets had been received. [52]

The draft recommendations for the observance of Armistice Day 1924 give a good impression of its breadth and scope:

> That the two minutes' silence at 11.00am should be observed throughout the Empire and that the Secretary of State for the Colonies and India should be requested to

The Cenotaph unveiled. Q31490.

invite the co-operation of the Dominion, Colonies and India as in previous years. Local Authorities in the United Kingdom would be requested, through the Press, to suspend all vehicular traffic between 11.00am and 11.02am, but rail and water transport would not be suspended. [53]

Before the temporary Cenotaph had been dismantled the Office of Works had had to insert a notice in the press to prevent the further accumulation of flowers there before work began. [54] The permanent version continued to surprise. The quantity of wreaths laid at its base bore immediate witness to its success, and in the early months they even threatened to hamper the flow of traffic. Between September 1923 and May 1932, 11,097 wreath frames were collected for re-use. [55] It soon became the custom for men to raise their hats when passing the monument. It may have declined a little as the years went by, for when in 1923 six MPs wrote to *The Times* on the question of the Cenotaph's illumination, they took the opportunity to record their wish that 'the very general practice of saluting the Cenotaph may be extended'. [56] Yet others declared that the custom was as strong as ever. [57]

> I never pass the Cenotaph without seeing men in all grades of life lifting their hats in reverence as they pass, even in the pouring

rain or inside a bus or car. [58]

> It is the only monument in London which passers-by naturally and of their own accord salute. [59]

Even a decade later the Cenotaph retained its impressive symbolism:

> The constant pile of wreaths and the continual saluting of it by passers-by on foot or in vehicles, testify to the hold it preserves. [60]

> When you think of the labour of love that the Cenotaph has been, and how it is the new symbol of all the Empire's hopes and yearning... [61]

The very real establishment of the Cenotaph in popular culture is revealed by the many and varied examples of the ways in which it was used as a symbol. The Office of Works soon found itself beset by instances of the memorial's 'unofficial use' by groups and individuals. Once again, the authorities seem to have been unprepared both for the depth and for the range of meanings the Cenotaph now assumed. Its strangely hybrid origins – a mixture of the official and the spontaneous – caused the Cenotaph to lead something of a double life.

Instances of usage over and above the original specification for the Cenotaph seem not to have occurred until some years after the war. At the 1922 Armistice Day ceremony 25,000 unemployed ex-servicemen paraded past the Cenotaph with their service medals hanging from red banners and pawn tickets pinned to their lapels. At this time the First Commissioner began to be concerned by individual 'appropriation' of the monumental site:

> I resent the idea that any individual can seize upon good places and retain them apparently for all time; [62]

and now specified that wreaths laid there should only commemorate those who had lost their lives in the Great War, and not be allowed for political or other purposes. [63] With reference to a contemporary incident concerning an unsuitable wreath, Aylmer Clerk cautioned both against allowing the Cenotaph to become the immediate centre of an unseemly public wrangle, and against allowing such free usage in the future:

> I shudder to think of the use to which the Cenotaph will certainly be put as and when the General Election takes place. [64]

In May 1933, a wreath laid at the Cenotaph by Rosenberg, Hitler's Ambassador to Britain, was thrown in the Thames. The culprit was fined. The wreath was replaced, though its swastika had been prudently removed. [65] By 1933 the Office had established a daily examination of the wreaths, at which controversial inscriptions were singled out. [66]

In 1939 the Office received a warning that wreaths had been 'laid in memory of persons killed in the International Brigade of the Spanish Republican Government...' and that the British Battalion of the International Brigade returned from Spain had organised a march of 300 members to the Cenotaph which had been stopped by police. Similar incidents in Liverpool suggested that 'an organised system of propaganda' was in operation. [67]

In 1946 the British League of Ex-Service Men and Women 'applied for permission to lay a wreath in memory of the British Armed Forces killed by Jewish Terrorists in Palestine'. The Office of Works, wise now to the political arena in which the Cenotaph operated, sought the advice of the Home Office, which cautioned against the potential publicity the Fascist organisation could draw out of such an event. [68]

As early as August 1919 the Office of Works was receiving requests to reproduce the Cenotaph, either in miniature, or on a large (if not full) scale. An employer of disabled servicemen sought the sole right to reproduce the Cenotaph in miniature. The Falcon Pottery of Stoke-on-Trent wanted to reproduce it in porcelain, another firm to make it in 'Fibrous Plaster'; Raphael Tuck to sell postcards of the Cenotaph, others to reproduce bronze or small silver models. [69] The Office of Works referred applicants to Lutyens, 'who has already expressed strong objections to the reproduction of his design in any form'. The writer added that though the models were 'hopeless travesties' he doubted whether the architect's objections would have any effect. [70]

The Cenotaph soon became the model, in form and name, for war memorials throughout Britain and the Commonwealth. [71] 'We are told that throughout England most communities are erecting Cenotaphs. I would be pleased to get some particulars as to their character' came the query from the Isle of Man. [72] A firm of solicitors from Bangor asked whether the design 'is the property of the Office of Works? Is it available for use elsewhere?' [73] All requests, which came from as far afield as the West African Frontier Force in the Gambia, the Agent General for Queensland, and the Governor of Hong Kong, were referred to Lutyens. [74] A letter that Lutyens wrote to Earle regarding a request to erect a replica in Rhode Island suggests that he was not opposed to the reproduction of his design – 'We should of course have no objection to a replica, provided you are willing to grant the request' at [75] – and he approved London (Ontario)'s request at a fee of £110.47.

In asking for permission to reproduce the Cenotaph on the appeal bill for their own War Memorial, Fulham Town Hall clearly recognised the authority of its image. [76]

The BBC had requested permission each year to broadcast the ceremony on the wireless, but had been repeatedly turned down. In 1928 the Office relented – ('BBC assure us that there will not be the slightest sound') – and were happy enough with the results to allow the ceremony to be filmed by British Movietone News the following year. By 1932 there were 10 official cine-photographers, along with 29 still photographers and 54 press representatives. The framework for the most effective dissemination of the Cenotaph and all that it was meant to stand for was now firmly in place. [77]

Decisions reached after the Second World War that the Cenotaph should commemorate another generation's war dead further invested this modest

Laying wreaths at the Cenotaph. Q45814.

'vessel' with significance. It became a symbol of extraordinary range.

In a draft press communiqué put out in October 1945 by the Home Office we read that the King had decided that Armistice Day 1945 should follow the lines adopted up to 1938, and that the Government had decided to look at the fixing of a Day of Remembrance for both the wars. [78] In Parliamentary Question Time the following month the Prime Minister was asked 'if he will consider adding the years 1939-45 to the Cenotaph... and making 11 November a Day of Remembrance for both wars'. [79] In June 1946 it was agreed that the Sunday before 11 November should be known as Remembrance Sunday [80] and in July that the inscription 'XXXIX-XLV' be added to 'The Glorious Dead MCMXIX'. [81] On 10 November 1946 the Cenotaph was unveiled for a third time. [82]

The Cenotaph is still a symbol with an unusually broad audience. Though its official symbolism is less powerful to today's general public, its functional significance has not altered. The Armistice Day ceremonies continue with little superficial change, and the regular day-to-day maintenance of the Cenotaph continues along with that of the capital's other statues. The only records as yet available pertaining to the Cenotaph after 1946 are thoroughly routine. In 1958 a car smashed the barrier. In 1967 £175/2/6d was spent annually on cleaning and renewing the flags every three weeks. Further, the monument was hosed down once a year, the lower part washed every fortnight and the steps and surround swept every other day. In 1968 the Cenotaph underwent a programme of restoration. [83]

In contrast to this trivia, the affair that blew up over Michael Foot's casual appearance at the 1981 Remembrance Day Ceremony revealed how much significance the Cenotaph still possesses. The catalyst of the debate was Foot's perceived violation of the norms of remembrance as enshrined in the Cenotaph ceremony. Despite the succession of stereotypical descriptions, the real issue emerged as being Foot's right to speak for the working class, with its corollary the Tory claim to the national past. The debate's very axis brought to the fore once again the unresolved question of the Cenotaph's ownership. Was this 'accidental' monument brought into being by the people, or by their rulers; and in whose control does it now lie?

The difference between two definitions of the Cenotaph, given in answer to two very similar questions, asked at fifty years' interval, gives another answer. In 1919 a Parliamentary Question had been asked rhetorically:

What is the object of erecting a Cenotaph?

and the answer provided

I presume the object is twofold; a) for the laying of wreaths, and b) that future generations shall know what has taken place now. [84]

In 1967, when asked for the official definition of the Cenotaph, the Office of Works offered the following:

The Cenotaph is a public statue authorised by section 2 of the Public Statues (Metropolis) Act 1854. [85]

Notes

The series of archives WORK 20 and 21 are deposited in the Public Record Office at Kew.

1. WORK 21/74

2. Ibid, 27 May 1919, Earle noted his comment on Derby's letter. Sir Lionel Earle (1866-1948) was appointed by Asquith as Permanent Secretary to the Office of Works in 1912, where he remained until his retirement in 1933. Earle's artistic interests are credited for the influence he brought to bear in the regulation of the memorials which were erected after the war. Edward Stanley (1865-1948) succeeded to his earldom in 1908. He became ambassador in Paris in January 1918 after serving in the War Office.

3. Ibid, Peace Celebration Committee.

4. Ibid, idem, 7 July 1919.

5. Alfred Mond, first Baron Melchett (1869-1930), industrialist, served as First Commissioner of Works from 1916 to 1921 in Lloyd George's coalition ministry. In 1913 Edwin Lutyens (1869-1944) had been appointed, with Herbert Baker, as architect to the New Delhi planning commission. Construction, delayed by the war, was not completed until 1930, and necessitated Lutyens's presence in India during the construction of the Cenotaph. The dating of Lutyens's initial involvement varies according to the source. Eric Homberger suggests that Lutyens was first asked to design the Cenotaph in early July (Mary Lutyens includes the possibility of late June), that is after the Committee meeting of 1 July. Homberger writes that Lutyens was summoned to 10 Downing Street in early July and the same day completed a sketch for the chief of the Office of Works. As *The Times* report dates from 8 July, this would mean that Lutyens completed the project within a week. Eric Homberger, 'The Story of the Cenotaph', *Times Literary Supplement*, 12 November 1976, p 1430. However, in the entry for the first sketch (from the Imperial War Museum) of the Cenotaph in the catalogue of the Arts Council exhibition, *Edwin Lutyens*, pp 148-9, we read that it bears the date 4 June 1919. Gavin Stamp writes, 'Lloyd George saw Lutyens early in June and told him that a "catafalque" was required in Whitehall... and Lutyens produced a sketch... that same day'. Mary Lutyens suggests that the name Cenotaph arose from her father's recollection of a stone seat that he

had designed for Gertrude Jekyll which had been nick-named the *Cenotaph of Sigismunda*. Although Lutyens preferred the title cenotaph to catafalque, there is not a great difference in their definitions. Cenotaph has more precise linguistic derivations, and indicates a burial monument without a burial, while catafalque denotes a temporary tomb-like structure used in funeral ceremonies.

6. WORK 21/74.

7. Ibid.

8. In Haig's case some persuasion was needed. He had earlier said, 'I have no intention of taking part in any triumphal ride with Foch, or with any pack of foreigners, through the streets of London, mainly in order to add to L.G.'s importance and help him in his election campaign'. Quoted by Homberger, op cit, p 1429.

9. WORK 21/74.

10. WORK 20 1/3, Office of Works to General Officer Commanding, 21 July 1919.

11. Ibid, Frank Baine to Bright, 23 July 1919.

12. Ibid, Earle to First Commissioner, 24 July 1919.

13. WORK 20/139, War Cabinet 602, 30 July 1919.

14. Idem.

15. Westminster Council agreed to the site on 13 August 1919, WORK 20/139

16. WORK 20 1/3.

17. WORK 20/139.

18. Ibid, Hansard, 9 December 1919.

19. Ibid, 29 July 1919.

20. H Avray Tipping, 'The Whitehall Cenotaph', *Country Life*, XLVI, 2 August 1919, pp 131.

21. WORK 20 1/2.

22. Its Chairman assured Earle that 'Whatever is done will be done on straightforward principles, and that only the wood actually used for the Cenotaph will be employed'. Ibid, 23 January 1920.

23. WORK 20/139, 28 August 1919.

24. Ibid, 8 January 1920.

25. Ibid.

26. WORK 20 1/2, 4 December 1919.

27. Ibid, 2 December 1919.

28. WORK 21/74, February 1924.

29. Ibid, 3 February 1924.

30. WORK 20 1/3, Baine to Bright, 23 July 1919.

31. WORK 20/139.

32. Ibid.

33. H Avray Tipping op cit, p 133.

34. WORK 20/139, 12 November 1919.

35. WORK 20 1/3.

36. WORK 20/139.

37. Ibid, in a letter to Mond, 1 November 1919.

38. WORK 20 1/3, 19 February 1920.

39. Ibid, 5 July 1920.

40. Ibid, 4 August 1920.

41. WORK 20/139, *Evening Standard*, 18 June 1923.

42. Ibid, *Daily News*.

43. WORK 20 1/3.

44. WORK 20 1/3, Assistant Secretary, Office of Works, 19 December 1919.

45. Submitted 16 April 1920, the lowest of eight quotations 8/5 WORK 20.

46. WORK 20/139, 'The Story of the Cenotaph as told by Sir Edwin Lutyens'.

47. Ibid, Lutyens to Earle, 19 September 1919.

48. WORK 20 1/3, 28 September 1920.

49. Ibid, 11 October 1920.

50. At first the Cabinet decided in favour of an anthem, followed by a hymn, one minute's silence, and 'The Last Post', decreeing that this be enacted 'wherever suitable throughout the Empire'. Ibid, 14 October 1920.

51. Ibid, 15 October 1920.

52. Ibid.

53. WORK 21/113, these date from 1924, but are included as a typical example, the minutiae of the celebrations varying little, if at all, from year to year.

54. WORK 20/139, 8 January 1920.

55. WORK 21/74, 9 June 1932.

56. WORK 20/139, 16 June 1923.

57. The *Glasgow Herald's* correspondent maintained: 'Though quibblers contend that London's lack of respect for her great memorial is amply demonstrated by a growing disinclination to bare the head in passing, the reverence is undiminished'. Ibid.

58. WORK 21/74, February 1924.

59. G S Cooper, *The Outdoor Monuments of London*, London, (1928), p. 20.

60. WORK 21/74, *The Scotsman*, 13 May 1933.

61. WORK 20/139, *The People*, 18 January 1925.

62. WORK 21/74, 15 June 1922.

63. Ibid, 3 July 1922.

64. WORK 21/74, Clerk to Earle, 10 July 1922.

65. The Office of Works received letters in support of the perpetrator, a Captain Sears. Ibid.

66. Ibid, 18 May 1933.

67. Ibid, Geoffrey Hutchinson to Sir Philip Sassoon, 13 January 1939.

68. Ibid, letter to Departmental Secretary of 5 December 1946.

69. Examples from WORK 20/205,

dating from 1 August 1919 to 14 February 1920.

70. Ibid, reply of 12 January 1921 to request from Ayles, Hants of 3 January 1921.

71. The Cenotaph was not a precocious war memorial; memorials were under discussion by 1915, and in December of that year the Civic Arts Association was founded to advise on design. From 1916 on there were regular competitions, conferences and publications on the subject.

72. WORK 20/205, 25 June 1920.

73. Ibid, 26 November 1919.

74. Ibid, 27 November 1919, n.d., 9 March 1920, 16 March 1921, 30 May 1928 and 14 April 1921 respectively.

75. Ibid, 19 June 1925.

76. Ibid, n.d.

77. WORK 21/113.

78. WORK 21/127.

79. Captain Bullock, 12 November 1945, WORK 20/206.

80. WORK 20/206, 16 June 1946.

81. Ibid, suggestion of 14 June 1946.

82. WORK 20/139 'The Story of the Cenotaph'.

83. WORK 20/267.

84. WORK 20/139, Sir F Banbury, Hansard, 9 December 1919.

85. WORK 20/267.

Acknowledgements

This article is a revised version of a text published for Stuart Brisley and Maya Balcioglu's *Cenotaph Project* by Orchard Gallery, Derry, in 1991.

Gassed and its detractors: interpreting Sargent's major war painting

John Thomas

John Thomas is a specialist in ecclesiastical art and architecture.

John S Sargent's large war painting *Gassed* has in recent years attracted two negative critical evaluations, the first as part of a detailed article in which another First World War painting (C R W Nevinson's *The Harvest of Battle*,1919) also figures; the second, in a brief paragraph introducing a book on war art.

Gassed is a wide panoramic picture (90 x 240 inches) in which two groups of gassed soldiers, their eyes bandaged due to the effects of gas, are being led by orderlies along a path made of wooden boarding. In front of the main group (which moves, procession-like, across the picture space, left to right) there is a crowd of similarly-affected soldiers lying on the ground. The second group of victims, also walking on boards, form the middle-ground of the space; both groups are seemingly heading for the same destination, probably a treatment tent. The picture recedes into a far distance where the moon is rising; the sun is setting, in the right-hand side, beyond the picture space. A group of footballers is seen playing, remote from the viewer, and there are some tents. Even further away, in the sky, several aeroplanes circle in dog fights. The group of gassed men furthest from the viewer are proceeding at an oblique angle. The destination of both groups is beyond the pictorial space, on the far right.

Jon Bird's article 'Representing the Great War' (published 1980)[1] sees Sargent's intention as that of glorifying the soldiers and their work, and as suggesting that all will eventually be well with them. They 'move towards… care, healing, security and safety, to be followed by a return to the state signified by the distant footballers flooded with light – rest, relaxation, leisure.'[2] Further, Bird sees the soldiers' progress as an echo of Christian iconography: the narrow, straight road leading eventually to redemption. The artist's ideology and visual message is seen to be the essentially feudal language of Arthurian legend.[3] In an earlier passage, Bird considered that the kind of people who appreciated such works as *Gassed* (it was exhibited from 1920 to 1923 at the Crystal Palace) were motivated by excessive jingoistic idealisation of the war ('the Great Adventure'[4]) and that such people employed a continued use of the rhetoric of Tennyson and Rider Haggard.[5] Bird's concerns are to expose the 'ideological position' of these two representations (Sargent's and Nevinson's) and to reveal the 'determining influence of the signifying practice and our construction as subjects within class, within culture,within language.'[6]

Gassed cases lying in the open at a Casualty Clearing Station. E(AUS) 4852.

The structure of the picture, the picture space, and the viewer's placing in respect of the subject by the way of this structure, 'the Quattrocento system – a single viewing eye, static ends centrally positioned – [suggests that] a Utopian code is being projected onto reality; a vision of clarity and order…' Bird considers that the perspectival system and viewpoint determine the viewer's ideological approach to the subject, creating idealisation (of the events and the men) rather than supposed realism: 'It would be hard to argue that either *Gassed* or *Harvest of Battle* are "realist" works. Although both… derive from specific concrete situations and are marked by the desire for verisimilitude, both universalise their themes.' [8] That what deceivingly masquerades as a work of grim realism is in the truth a rhetorical idealisation of soldiers' suffering, seems to be the Bird's principal objection to *Gassed*.

The second objection to the painting appears to be from a completely different angle. In the 'Author's Note' to his *Art and War: Twentieth Century Warfare as Depicted by War Artists* (1990) [9] M R D Foot explains that his book has omitted a few pictures by now so well known that they verge on the hackneyed – among them, Sargent's *Gassed*. 'I have a second, stronger reason for omitting *Gassed*: not only is it hackneyed, but it gives a false impression. My own father once stood in one of those pathetic-seeming queues of men blinded by mustard gas, each with his hand on the shoulder of the man in front; was back in action with his battery a week later; and ever thereafter praised mustard gas, which seldom killed anybody, as a humane weapon.' Where one author objects to Sargent's (supposed) production of a false, ultimately rosy image, the other complains of the portrayal of greater-than-realistic suffering and horror.

While Jon Bird is highly informative on the

details of the commission and the commissioners, and the work's early reception (both documented in detail in Imperial War Museum records), he gives no information about the place of *Gassed* in Sargent's work, nor the circumstances that produced the picture; Bird's evaluation of *Gassed* disregards the context of the work, both artistically, and in terms of the artist's experience.[10]

John Singer Sargent (1856-1925) was recruited as an official war artist in May/June 1918. [11] Sargent had been given the specific commission (by the British War Memorials Committee) to produce a depiction of the American forces working in co-operation with their British allies (America entered the war in April 1917, and the American soldiers took their place in the battle line in May 1918). This request surely derived from Sargent's unusual position of being an artist strongly wedded to his American citizenship, yet also a long-time resident of Britain, and a part of the London artistic establishment and the foremost portraitist of British high society. Sargent clearly took his instructions very seriously – as an artist used to working to the requests of his client – and went to much trouble, driving round the war zones of France, trying to catch up with the American forces. One other idea was clearly central in his mind, that of painting not a few of these co-operating allies, but great bodies of men, a crowd scene, rather than isolated combatants. The source of this – and large masses of people had not hitherto formed an important concern in Sargent's artistic aims – seems to have come from the Ministry of Information's desire for an epic.[12] But it has also been connected with the commission that had been at the forefront of Sargent's mind since 1890, the set of murals for the Boston Public Library on the theme *The Triumph of Religion*. These are filled with many friezes of figures, and the central group of gassed men has been understood as a reflection of such groups as the frieze of prophets (1895)[13], (though a closer parallel with the prophets is seen in the less-than-inspiring group portrait of Britain's military leaders, *Some General Officers of the Great War* [1920-22, National Portrait Gallery, London]; the generals, like the prophets, face the viewer).

From Charing Cross station (2 July 1918), Sargent went to Boulogne, and was soon attached to the Guards Division, whose HQ was at Bavincourt, south of Arras. He then moved with the Guards into the battle line, to their HQ near Berles au Bois. Here he was joined by his friend Professor Henry Tonks, of the Slade School of Art, on 16 July. Later, they went to Arras itself, where Sargent painted the ruined cathedral.[14] For a while Sargent's efforts to find a suitable subject – ideally large numbers of American and British troops in action – were frustrated, and so instead he produced a number of watercolours and sketches.

Another recent article concerned with First World War art examines the reaction of almost paralysis, that the experience of war zone *landscape*, had upon the war artists. 'Out of a Vortex, Into a Void' (1991, by Paul Gough) [15] quotes Sargent's words concerning the 'scattered' and 'meagre' nature of the shattered environment (from Sargent's letter to Evan Charteris of 11 September 1928).[16] But Gough seems to attribute Sargent's inability to find a suitable subject to this reaction to these circumstances, failing to report the artist's instructions and aims. In fact, certain drawings in the Corcoran Gallery of Art, Washington DC, show that Sargent *was* drawn to trying to depict the devastated scenes in which he vainly looked for his epic. [17]

On 21 August, however, late in the afternoon, Sargent and Tonks heard that the Guards were advancing, and followed them in a motor car. They also heard, according to Tonks, that some victims of gas attacks had been taken to a Casualty Clearing Station on the Arras-Doullens road, where they were to receive treatment (specifically, at Le Bac du Sud, according to the painting's sub-title, in Charteris's inventory). Such an opportunity was important to Tonks as he had been commissioned to produce a work on a medical theme. [18] There, as the sun began to sink, they discovered the scene later depicted in *Gassed*, and Sargent made several sketches in pencil and charcoal, and various notes. [19] Tonks readily consented to Sargent making this subject his own; however, Sargent continued to seek out other suitable scenes, and spent the rest of August and September with an American unit near Ypres, and later (24 September onwards) sketching at a POW camp near Péronne. Then – having caught the flu – he was sent to a casualty-clearing station near Roisel, and spent a week in bed. Tonks later found similar medical subjects, and produced *An Advanced Dressing Station In France* (IWM). [20]

Sargent returned to London late in October, and began painting in his Fulham Road studio. A photograph dated 27 May 1918 shows groups of gassed soldiers lying in groups in a field, beside a road. While there are fewer victims than in Sargent's work, and none walking, it shows the men assuming precisely the same attitudes as seen in the painting. [21] In the photograph, the road, with its lining of trees and vehicles, is in the background: Sargent presumably had the Arras-Doullens road behind him. A further photograph, of the same date, shows a group of at least twelve gas victims, their hands resting on the shoulder of the man in front, again, as in the painting. Here, the men are very close together, walking with much smaller steps. [22] While Sargent did use photographs of subjects, there is no suggestion of his taking any on this occasion. However, he did make use of models in the studio.

Accounts of Sargent and his work testify to his foremost, lifelong, concern to use his art to produce a record of an actual scene in his view. It is not sufficient to note the claim that he painted what he saw on this occasion, for the depiction of external reality was essential to his understanding of his art. This approach was surely a product of his training in the French academic tradition (with an influence of Barbizon naturalism), which involved emphasis on spontaneity, encouraged by his teacher Emile Carolus-Duran, and may go back to the youthful sketching of places and things observed that filled many hours during his endless trekking around the cities, spas and resorts of Europe, in the train of his restless, rootless, parents. [23] Accounts have recorded Sargent's rather boyish exercises in putting his skills to the test. In his Broadway sojourns (mid-1880s) he would emerge from the house with an easel, wander around in circles for a while, then set about recording whatever chanced into his view. [24] It was absolutely necessary, of course, that *Gassed* be produced in the studio (and indeed, his early landscapes were not necessarily the *au plein air* pictures they might appear). The concern to produce a faithful record of the scene can be noted in the attention given to the details of the soldiers' uniforms, which are particularly prominent in the charcoal sketches.

The first type of gas (January 1915), was a simple tear gas ('lachrymatory' as contemporary accounts have it), followed by chlorine (April 1917). Also, the devices for deploying the weapons ('delivery systems' might be the modern parlance) increased in sophistication. It is clear from records, however, that victims could receive exceedingly mild doses (from clouds that lingered long in hollows, woods, or trenches, or from leaking canisters which they were manhandling, gas intended for the enemy, not themselves) with minimal effects, as suggested by the testimony of Foot senior, who was not alone in claiming that gas was a humane weapon. [25]

The symptoms of mustard gas poisoning generally took two-to-three hours to be felt, and began with irritation of the eyes, resulting in conjunctivitis. Next, the nose would run with mucous, as with a heavy cold, which would be followed by nausea and vomiting. Finally, the eyelids would swell, causing complete closure of the palpebral fissure. This process might take as long as twenty-four hours, and be accompanied by pus running down the cheek. The vocal cords were also immobilised, to a greater or lesser extent, and a severe burning in the throat created an excessive thirst. Any areas of the skin exposed to the gas – or, worse still, the liquid that produced the gas – would be badly burned, causing a red/purple effect. Often the genitals were severely damaged by burning, and one theory for the occurence of burning in non-exposed areas was the presence of hair and with it sebum, which was said to aggravate the destructive effects of the chemical. In the second twenty-four hours, blisters would form, the ears might swell, the genitals might be entirely destroyed, and the victim would cough up shreds of necrosed mucous membrane. Mucous might take the form of false membrane in the lungs and bronchi, and on at least one occasion, a victim brought up a tree-like cast of the bronchi, some hours before expiring. In essence, mustard gas killed by destroying the respiratory tracts, by causing acute septic bronchi-pneumonia, with emphysema and other complications. Death was known to have occurred between two and ten days. [26]

This information is drawn from official records; a more graphic account of a gas victim is given in Wilfred Owen's 'Dulci et Decorum Est':

> …flound'ring like a man in fire or lime…
> …guttering, choking, drowning.
> …the white eyes writhing in his face,
> His hanging face, like a devil's sick of sin;
> …the froth corrupted-lungs,
> Obscene as cancer, bitter as the cud
> Of vile, incurable sores on innocent tongues…

But what is the precise nature of the fate suffered by the men in this painting? 1918 saw some of the most intense gas attacks mounted against British troops, and by this time, as has been noted, the most lethal form (mustard gas) was being deployed. By late 1917, a chain of services had been established by the army medical authorities, including regimental aid posts, field ambulances, casualty clearing stations, and finally, base hospitals. With earlier gas weapons there had been a need, from the first sign of effects, to keep victims in a recumbent position; but with mustard gas, cases were generally able to walk, initially, but needed careful handling once bronchial damage set in. A crucial treatment was to supply victims with oxygen, which by this stage of the war was the role of the Casualty Clearing Stations. [27]

Certainly the victims depicted in the painting have suffered more than the minimal exposure referred

to above. Each man's eyes have been bandaged with lint, probably at the field ambulance. As it is impossible to know when gas was deployed against the Guards, we cannot estimate how long the substance has been taking effect, but, being late in the day, it is probably for some hours. The seeming collapse towards death suggested by some of the victims is complemented, however, by the odd appearance of one soldier (bottom, right) who is able to prop himself up on his left elbow, and drink from a canteen. But most of the others seem to be in a very bad state. What is the relationship between the two groups? Are those on the ground simply waiting their turn for treatment in a tent (the view of Charles Merrill Mount [28]), towards which the walking men appear to be heading? (Tonks [first account, Note 20] seems to suggest that Sargent depicted groups being led to the field, there to lie down.) Or are there two degrees of severity of casualty seen in those lying, and those walking? One requirement of the medical services was that they quickly distinguished between the severity of cases brought in, to see which victims might respond to treatment, and which were more severely affected.

Certainly, as depicted, the soldiers on the ground form a strong contrast with those few who are walking. This apparent distinction makes the painting more powerful, for the men who appear to have fallen towards death far outnumber those on their feet. We

realise that the large scale of the work, and the relatively low viewpoint, serve the purpose of making the fallen have a visual impact that more than equates them with the walking. The viewpoint makes the walking men seem much larger than life (and, Bird might consider, supposedly heroic, idealised); but they also have the stiff, awkward gait of the newly-blind. The bare-headed man, third from left, may seem to have a proud bearing, but he is simply holding his head in a fixed manner sometimes exhibited by the blind, whose heads do not have to move around to look at things. They move with their legs jerking forward, like puppets (the third victim from the right, on being told of a step, has raised his foot far higher than necessary, as blind people sometimes do, when warned of approaching steps).

If they are heroic or idealised, it is in the image of some tragic chorus. The soldiers' pathetic staggering produces the effect of a kind of dance of death – enhanced by the rhythm set up by the different postures – no figure is identical, yet each is given a slightly swaying stance, made more pronounced by the bowed heads.

The vigorous, formal composition suggests such precedents as I E Repin's Volga *Bargemen* (1870; Russian Museum, St Petersburg [29]), in which a clutch of suffering men strain against the weight of their burden. Frank Brangwyn's lithograph *Platelayers* (c 1906 [30]) depicts six railway labourers straining, with levers, to move a length of rail, their bodies bent and heads bowed with effort. This line of men is set almost frontally to the viewer, unlike Repin's bargemen. A group of men, more in anguish than bent by burdens, is seen – in three-dimensional form – in Rodin's *Burghers of Calais* (1886; Calais and London [31]), figures whose forms have a certain similarity, perhaps, with the walking gas victims. A much larger group, indeed procession, of people with heads bowed and faces covered, is seen in Courbet's *Burial at Ornans* (1849 [33]), which was acquired by the Louvre in 1882, when Sargent was still in Paris. Another comparison (made by Richard Ormond) is with Sargent's somewhat curious group of women (or rather, the same model depicted repeatedly) promenading draped in shawls, *Cashmere* (c 1908; private collection). A frieze of soldiers, marching or standing-easy, was often to be sculpted – in low relief – on the panels of war memorials, the men seen in profile, a formalised, version of Sargent's composition. [33]

In the principal walking group, the leader is in khaki, not white (in Mount's account, some of the leaders were officers, and some medical orderlies [34]). This leader is looking backwards, while still holding the waist of the man in front, and so his body, including the neck, is portrayed with marked torsion. With this man's backward look, if, like Bird, we choose to seek a Biblical image, it is surely that of the blind leading the blind that most readily comes to mind. In the whole painting, only one figure (the orderly at the front, in the rear group) is actually shown with eyes looking to the common destination (the orderly at the rear of this group may have his eyes lowered, as he tends a vomiting victim; his face is barely depicted, in the indistinct, undetailed manner that Sargent occasionally employed for human features in his Impressionist phase (1880s) [35]. The bandaged soldiers must be seen to be related to the large number of hooded, draped, cloaked, and turbaned figures (often denied vision of the outer world) that feature in Sargent's oeuvre. The physical 'gesture', found at the front of the principal group, is noticeably not pointing forward to the intended destination, but an arm hanging down in pathetic resignation.

Although we are right to avoid the now over-loaded words 'realism' or 'realistic', *Gassed* should be seen as an overpowering and accurate display of the real horror of modern war (as relevant, in this age of the deployment of chemical weapons, as ever it was in 1918). The footballers provide an added irony: they are not just off-duty Tommies briefly kicking a ball about in a respite from war. They are dressed in proper football kit, for someone has organised a game yards from where the players' comrades are writhing in agony or dying. The aeroplanes in the distance suggest future (more mechanised) wars, war going on for ever.

Avoiding the interpretation of horror requires us to dismiss the evident misery and suffering displayed by both the fallen, and walking, figures. Foot does this, not only by denying the suffering, but by dismissing the picture as 'hackneyed', seeming to appeal to some Berger-like argument of the degradation of images and their meaning by way of trivialising mass-reproduction in inappropriate settings. Yet the reproductions printed in books on Sargent rarely do justice to such a vast work. Bird tries to do the same by turning the oft-repeated story of the woman who fainted on seeing the painting (her brother had recently perished in the war from the effects of gas) into a fit of some kind of jingoistic sexual hysteria – surely a dubious mode of interpreting human behaviour. [36]

Rather, it should be considered that Sargent used his very considerable skills to present a horrific display of hideous suffering in a way that is very moving through its power, scale, and pictorial viewpoint. Sargent did not portray soldiers in any of his war paintings as heroic, noble, proud, or bound for any glorious destiny. When he did find a troop of men and equipment, moving to the front (*The Road*, 1918; Museum of Fine Arts, Boston [37]), it was at night, and the men (Americans and British, probably) seem to be marching grimly (through rain?), with only darkness around them. Even the idealised symbolic mural *The Americans coming to Europe* (1922; staircase of the Widener Library, Harvard University [38]) shows the ranks of men reaching out to give aid to their war-ravaged allies; there is an eagle and a Stars & Stripes, but it is hardly an orgy of unrestrained patriotism.

Gassed is the obverse of beauty and splendour. Sargent's lush Edwardian sensuality and aestheticism is here turned to the service of the very opposite kind of image from that for which it had developed. The same qualities and skills are here seen to display the portrayal of suffering and death just as effectively as, previously, they had provided a lavish vision of opulence and grandeur. Ironically, perhaps, it can be suggested that such art has actually expressed the horrific far more truthfully and effectively than the aesthetics of Expressionism, Cubism, Dadaism and so forth which are often considered necessary – new means, for a new age of evil – to do this work. Nevinson's *Returning to the Trenches* (1914–5; National Gallery of Canada, Ottawa [39]) shows a mass of soldiers struggling towards a common destination, but the Futurist techniques with which they

are depicted somehow de-humanise them – they are just a pattern of shapes.

What of Sargent's experience of the scene, and his feelings and reactions to war? This is the other side of the equation that has to balance, if the interpretation of *Gassed* as a moving portrayal of horror is to be accepted. All the biographical accounts stress the artist's complete naivety as to the war ('Do they fight on Sundays'?) the Great War as 'mere folly', and above all, an annoying inconvenience – he spent much of 1914 marooned in Austria. However it is clear that his feelings had hardened some time before he saw the scene depicted in *Gassed*, and Richard Ormond has referred to the preponderance, in his Austrian paintings, of images of crucifixes and confessionals.[40] The death of his niece Rose Marie (killed by German shells during a church service in Paris on 29 March 1918) contributed to this. Charteris recounts Sargent's experience (late September/early October – *after* seeing the victims beside the Doullens road) of lying in bed in a hospital tent during a bout of flu, listening to 'groans of wounded, and the chokings and coughing of gassed men, which was a nightmare'.

Such questions raise the greater issue of Sargent's emotional and spiritual make-up, and its role in his art. The biographical accounts pay little attention to his personal life, and his paintings are often seen to be lacking in expressions of feeling and human concern – perhaps a consequence of his abnormal childhood, and upbringing. Certainly he was possessed of considerable intellectual curiosity as well as gifted with the skills of music, and language-learning. Stanley Olson, for example, claims that Sargent possessed 'no religious feelings whatsoever'[42], yet did no influence of his father's lifelong Christian faith pass to him? Should Peter Burman's assessment of the powerful sculpture, *Crucifixion with Adam and Eve* (St Paul's Cathedral, London, and Boston Public Library) 'a deeply-felt religious work'[43] be rejected?

Jon Bird, in his interpretation linking the work to Christian doctrine, is certainly right in pointing to the fact that the group of soldiers are moving towards the light. It was – *in reality* – an exceptionally bright sun-filled evening, and rich pools of sunshine alight on to many planes of the objects depicted. It is a very different study-in-twilight from that captured in *Carnation, Lily, Lily, Rose* (1885-6; Tate Gallery, London), where dying light falls softly on children's faces and flowers. Army uniforms do not readily reflect light, but here, it shines with a curious yellow glow upon arms and legs, hats and sleeves. This is less the 'kindly light'[44] of J H Newman, or Owen[45], than the cruel apocalyptic light[46] of Edwin Muir. While it is obviously the end of the day, sometimes, when the painting is only seen in part – as one approaches the entrance to the Sargent Room – the scene can also have an odd quality of morning, the light of dawn. The light's source, we have noted, is beyond the picture space. Lines of tent guy-ropes (foreground, right) help to point towards the unseen destination; indeed, the ropes seem to fall either side of the temporary wooden path, and so may be the guys of the tent which the soldiers appear to be about to enter. Many accounts of the war – both literary and graphic – abound in images of eschatology and apocalypse, both explicit and by interpretation (eg a contemporary account of Nevison's *Harvest of Battle*, quoted by Bird [47]), and clearly the more pessimistic reflections on the war and its significance, at the time, saw it and the future of human history in just these terms.

The idea of endless war – suggested above – implied the eventual destruction of civilisation. As Owen wrote ('Strange Meeting'), 'None will break rank, though nations trek from progress', and this line surely gives meaning to the sinking sun, which suggests the setting sun of Empire, in its ideal form of civilisation, the European, Western dream of reason, order, truth, goodness and progress – 'Knowledge hand in hand with peace' [48] – once set to fill the earth, but now dying forever amidst its slaughtered sons. In this way, the painting can be seen as having a prophetic message to its time. We might see *Gassed* as a modern-day parable on the ancient theme of universal death, judgement, and the division into the saved and the damned. The latter are seen on the ground, men of the earth, about to sink through it to perpetual darkness beneath (they have a little of the grotesque tangle of human forms found in the Boston Public Library mural *Hell* – sketch dated c. 1903–9, painted 1895–1916 [49]). They, and the walking men, are truly in some no man's land of war, between this world and the next. The staggering men are still 'blinded' by 'death', but they, at least, are progressing towards the light of eventual salvation. Their helpers, leading them to the light, dare not yet look on it themselves, except for the leader of the rear group, who steadfastly has his face forward; dressed in white, he bears the red cross of some saintly, knightly order, on his sleeve; the destination is beyond the sight of also (in one of the sketches he also appears to be looking downwards [50]). The whole earthly realm is sinking to its end, and in the distance, far above and beyond the world, squadrons fight one another in some ultimate show-down of good and evil.

Gassed is a truly contemporary painting. We miss its message if we thoughtlessly consign its subject-matter to the dustbin of our memory of history – the victims of Saddam Hussein's gassing of Kurdish villages would testify to this sad fact. And thus the official artist of the 1991 Gulf War, John Keane, placed a postcard-reproduction of *Gassed* – the kind on sale at the IWM bookshop for 30 pence – in the corner of his painting *An Ecstacy of Fumbling*. [51] This work deals with a related theme, and the title comes from 'Dulci et Decorum Est' – the poem by Wilfred Owen, quoted above.

But *Gassed* is also timeless. An overriding reason for the lasting importance of the work is that its imagery can pass even beyond its own powerful subject-matter, of war and the pity of war, of death and the end of things, to speak of the perpetual human condition. A few may seem to hold some vision that bids them draw the bewildered members of their race onward; while a handful of others, oblivious to all that is real, dally in the sunshine, briefly, heedless of the approaching end.

Notes

1. Jon Bird, *Representing the Great War*, Block, London, (3), 1980, pp 41-52 (hereafter 'Bird').
2. Bird, p 49.
3. Ibid.
4. Bird, p 45.
5. Ibid.
6. Bird, p 51.
7. Bird, p 47.
8. Bird, p 51.
9. M R D Foot, *Art and War. Twentieth Century Warfare As Depicted by War Artists*, Headline/Imperial War Museum, 1990, p 7.
10. Accounts of Sargent's life and work include: Evan Charteris, *John Sargent*, Heinemann, London/Charles Scribner's, New York, 1927; Richard Ormond, *John Singer Sargent. Paintings, Drawings, Watercolours*, Phaidon, London, 1970; Carter Ratcliff, *John Singer Sargent*, Abbeyville Press, New York, 1982; Stanley Olson, *John Singer Sargent, His Portrait*, Barrie & Jenkins, London, 1986 (hearafter 'Charteris', 'Ormond', 'Ratcliff' and 'Olson'; other published works are cited below, Notes 18, 29, 36).
11. Charteris, pp 210, 211.
12. Ormond, p 87.
13. Ratcliff, p 203.
14. Ormond, p 133.
15. Paul Gough, 'Out of a Vortex, into a Void', *Times Higher Education Supplement*, 29 November 1991, p 16.
16. Charteris (letter to, of 11 September 1918), p 214.
17. 'Soldiers in a devastated Landscape' (1918, 49.142), and *verso*, 'Devastated Trees' illustrated in Edward J. Nygren, *John Singer Sargent. Drawings from the Cocoran Gallery of Art*, Smithsonian Institution and Corcoran Gallery of Art, Washington, 1983, p 100.
18. Sargent was reluctant to reveal the identity of the men depicted (Charteris, p 215), but Charteris writes (ibid) that it was the 99th and 8th Brigades of the 3rd Division of Guards, who moved through gas that was set in motion by the hot sun.
19. Two accounts of the artists' witnessing of the scene exist, both written by Tonks. One is in a letter (4 October 1918) to Alfred Yockney, secretary of the Memorial Committee: 'After luncheon we started out in Sargent's car together along the road to Doullens … The dressing Station was situated on the road and consisted of a number of huts and a few tents. Gassed cases kept coming in, led along in parties of about six just as Sargent has depicted them, by an orderly. They sat or lay down on the grass, there must have been several hundred, evidently suffering a great deal chiefly I fancy from their eyes which were covered up by a piece of lint. The gas was mustard gas … Sargent was very struck by the scene and immediately made a lot of notes. It was a very fine evening and the sun toward setting' (quoted by Ormond, p.258).
And Charteris quotes a lengthy account (source not given): 'Professor Tonks writes: … One day we heard that the Guards Division were advancing so we motored towards them to find materials for our subjects. We knew that a number of gassed men were being taken to a dressing station on the Doullens Road, so we went there in the evening. He immediately began making sketches and a little later asked me if I would mind his making this essentially medical subject his, and I told him I did not in the least mind. He worked hard and made a number of pencil and pen sketches which formed the bases of the oil painting known as *Gassed* now in the War Museum. It is a good representation of what we saw, as it gives a sense of the surrounding peace. I regret he did not put in something I noticed, a French boy and girl of about 8 years, who watched the procession of men with a certain calm philosophy for an hour or more, it made a strange contrast. 'Charteris, p. 212). Tonks's final suggestion is fascinating, as the presence of viewers internal to the picture – like a pair of putti, voyeuristically watching a Baroque Biblical scene – would have further drawn the viewer into the picture-space, and as Tonks realised, have emphasised the tragedy of the events and the madness of war. It is unfortunate that we have no account of the incident written by Sargent himself.
20. Joseph Hone, *The Life of Henry Tonks*, Heinemann, London, 1939, pp 142-5.
21. IWM photograph E(AUS). 4852.
22. IWM photograph Q. 11, 586.
23. Described in detail in Olson's first five chapters.
24. Olson, p 124.
25. C H Foulkes, *Gas! The Story of the Special Brigade*, Willam Blackwood, Edinburgh and London, 1934, pp29-, 66-84, 324-338, etc.
26. W G Macpherson, etc., eds, *Medical Services. Diseases of the War*, Vol II (History of the Great War. Based on Official Documents), HMSO, London, 1923, pp 428-441, 495-505, etc. Bird (his note 24) quotes the suitably gruesome account in Dennis Winter, *Death's Men. Soldiers of the Great War*, Penguin, Harmondsworth, 1978, p 122.
27. Official history cited Note 27, p 505-516.
28. Charles Merrill Mount, *John Singer Sargent. A biography*, The Cresset Press, London, 1957, p 295 (hereafter "Mount").
29. George Heard Hamilton, *The Art and Architecture of Russia*, Penguin, Harmondsworth, 2nd ed, 1975 (Pelican History of art), pp 265-6, pl 164.
30. Rodney Brangwyn, *Brangwyn*, William Kimber, London, 1978, facing p 193.
31. The similarity is more marked, perhaps, in the first (1884) moquette for the sculpture, in which the closely-grouped figures face the same direction (see Arts Council of Great Britain, 1974 (exhibition catalogue), item 36,p 50).
32. Arts Council of Great Britain, *Gustave Courbet, 1819-1877*, 1978 (exhibition catalogue), p 210.
33. For example Battle of Marne memorial (Gilbert Ledward) and the Stourbridge war memorial (John Cassidy), pls 179 and 183 respectively in Alan Borg, *War Memorials from Antiquity to the Present*, Leo Cooper, London, 1991; and the St. Anne's war memorial, Lytham St. Anne's (Walter Marsden), pl 182b, p100, in Derek Boorman, *At the Going Down of the Sun. British First World War Memorials*, William Sessions, The Ebor Press, York, 1988.
34. Mount, p 295.
35. For example, *A Backwater at Wargrave* (1887) and *By the River* (1888), pls 28 and 32 respectively in Stanley Olson, Warren Adelson and Richard Ormond, *Sargent at Broadway. The Impressionist Years*, Universe/Coe Kerr Gallery, New York/John Murray, London, 1986.
36. Bird, p 48.
37. Ratcliff, pl 301, p 201.
38. Ratcliff, pl 309, p 207. This uninspired work employed a single face – one model – for about thirty soldiers.
39. Dennis Farr, *English Art, 1870-1940*, Oxford University Press, Oxford, 1978 (Oxford History of English Art), pl 83A.
40. Ormond, p 77.
41. Charteris, p 216. Charteris's own evalation of the painting is, I consider, among the more accurate: 'There is no striving after the picturesque; dramatic account has been entirely dispensed with. It is stated in its starkest terms, it is more than merely descriptive. He has given a spiritual value to realism, and dignity and solemnity to the facts' (p 215).
42. Olson, p 269.
43. *St Paul's Cathedral*, Bell & Hyman, London, 1987 (New Bell's Cathedral Series), p 138.
44. 'Lead kindly light, amidst the encircling gloom, lead thou me on' (1833).
45. In 'Futility' Owen presents an image of the sun waking a man out of death: 'Move him into the sun -/Gently its touch awoke him once/ …If anything might arouse him now/The kind old sun will know'.
46. *Horses*, published 1925.
47. Bird, p 43, quoting a critic of the *Express*, 28 March 1919.
48. 'When knowledge hand in hand with peace,/Shall walk the earth abroad:/The day of perfect righteousness,/The promised day of God' – the 19th century myth of progress, here seen in its Christian form (F.L. Hosmer's *'Thy Kingdom come, on bended knee'*, 1891), but very similar ideas – peaceful progress to utopia – were expressed by socialists, imperialists, liberals, materialists, scientific rationalists, etc.
49. Ratcliff, pl 187, p 132.
50. 'An orderly lining up gassed soldiers', ART. 1612(9), pencil sketch.
51. John Keane told me that there was no significance to the fact that the postcard of *Gassed* was set upside down.

Acknowledgments

The author wishes to thank the following for their assistance, information, and advice, towards the production of this article: Jennifer Wood, Suzanne Bardgett, and Stephen Nash (Imperial War Museum), Roy Eyeions (Royal Army Medical Corps Historical Museum), library staff of the Royal College of Art and the University of London Library, Alan Barber, and especially, Mike Hazzledine (South Bank University).

Unknown pioneer: Edward Foxen Cooper and the Imperial War Museum Film Archive, 1919-1934

Roger Smither and David Walsh

Roger Smither is Keeper of the Department of Film. David Walsh is the Department's Deputy Preservation Officer.

The Imperial War Museum was conceived in 1917 as the nation's - soon redefined as the Empire's - memorial to the sacrifice and effort which the War had represented. Through its curator, Major Charles ffoulkes, the Museum expressed early concern that film be among the historical records to be permanently preserved. This was not a completely novel idea: there had been calls for the recognition of the historical value of film almost as soon as the first moving pictures had been projected, the best-known being a pamphlet published in Paris in March 1898 by the Polish cameraman Boleslaw Matuszewski which was actually entitled *Une nouvelle source de l'histoire.* If not novel, it was still an unusual suggestion - the medium of film was not merely new but in many eyes was perceived only as a low form of entertainment, 'an amusement fit for children and half-wits'. [1] What was more than unusual, however, was to see a Government-funded body acting on these suggestions. This was what happened when Major ffoulkes reported to the first meeting of the Board of Trustees after the Imperial War Museum Act (1920) brought the Museum into formal existence 'that the Treasury had instructed him to take over and preserve all War Cinematograph films and that a certain sum for this purpose had been allotted in the estimates for 1921-1922.' [2]

Behind this simple statement lay the beginnings of a remarkable achievement. Some fifteen years before the date normally recognised for the birth of the film archive movement, the Imperial War Museum was committing serious resources to the building of something that would unquestionably be recognised as a film archive by today's standards. The statutes of the International Federation of Film Archives (FIAF - itself founded in 1938) define the 'main object' of a member as being 'the collection, preservation, restoration and cataloguing of films'; members are also 'encouraged to organise the projection and the viewing of films'. [3] On behalf of Major ffoulkes and the Museum, a man named Edward Staple Foxen Cooper was seeking to address all of these issues (with the exception of 'restoration', which was, as we shall see, not at the time perceived as a priority) in the early post-war period.

Foxen Cooper was known even to his contemporaries as 'a Whitehall man of mystery', and piecing together the details of his career is not always easy. The only photograph of him that has come to light so far appears on the left. He was born on 16 April 1872, and started work as a mechanical engineering draughtsman for the Fire Brigade Department of the London County Council in 1898. He became an early expert in the special risks associated with the operation of the new medium of cinema, one account describing him as 'an inspector of theatres and music-halls'. Fire brigades were bound to be concerned about a form of public entertainment which brought together the powerful light sources needed for projection and cellulose nitrate, the material used in almost all professionally shown films until after the Second World War. Nitrate film is highly inflammable and the dangers were clear from the earliest days of the medium. More than a hundred people, including many society figures, had died when a fire broke out at a film showing at the Bazar de la Charité in Paris in May 1897. The Cinematograph Act of 1909 gave local authorities in Britain responsibility for licensing cinema premises. Foxen Cooper's career developed from specific fire-prevention concerns into general involvement in film matters.

In November 1915 his part-time services were placed at the disposal of the Board of Customs and Excise to advise the Board on cinematograph matters. The LCC agreed to continue this arrangement for four years but then demanded his immediate return to full duties in July 1919. Foxen Cooper preferred to resign from the Council. His services were by then also being used by the Foreign Office, which was eager to develop the use of film for propaganda purposes, and he had recognised status as the Government's 'adviser on cinematograph matters'. The role of part-time custodian to the Museum's film collection was at this point added to his other duties, and in November 1920 the Treasury formally recognised that the Museum should join with the Foreign Office and with Customs and Excise in paying his salary. [4]

Preserving an estimated 250,000 feet of film for posterity presented Foxen Cooper with an unprecedented task. Motion picture film in any form had only existed for 25 years and although the hazards of storing the dangerously inflammable cellulose nitrate film-stock were well recognised, very little thought had been given to safeguarding the images for the long term. Foxen Cooper approached the major film-stock manufacturers for advice and received from Kodak a set of recommendations which, for the most part, could happily form the basis of a conservation policy today. [5] In essence, they warned of the likelihood of films shrinking and becoming brittle with age, and of the danger of image loss due to poor fixing and washing. They therefore suggested the films should be refixed and thoroughly rewashed before being stored in cool conditions. They were careful to point out, however, that,

even if their recommendations were adhered to, the films would inevitably decompose slowly over the years. [6]

Foxen Cooper certainly seems to have taken their advice to heart, for in September 1920 he visited Aldershot to check on the condition of the films still in the hands of the War Office, stored at the Field Ordnance Depot. (At the same time, the Museum was gathering information about film held in the Admiralty, the Foreign Office and other Government Departments.) He was not entirely happy with what he found - negatives were showing 'considerable signs of wear, whilst others were slightly discoloured' (these were films which could have been no more than four years old). [7] In addition 'the temperature of the store was far too high, probably over 70° F, due to the steam heating apparatus being at work.' In his report back to Major ffoulkes, Foxen Cooper expressed concern about the high temperatures and the poor fire precautions - there were apparently over 500,000 ft of nitrate positives stored in the adjoining room - adding that 'it is essential that the negatives be again fixed and washed'.

A scene from *Gaumont Graphic* issue 962 – the newsreel coverage of the opening of the Imperial War Museum exhibition at Crystal Palace on 9 June 1920. A copy of this film was acquired for the Museum's own archive. FLM 2551

In October, Foxen Cooper drew up first year estimates for the task of preserving the Museum's films. [8] As well as a requirement for a small staff and some items of equipment, by far the largest element in the estimates was the provision for 'preservation work on the negatives and the printing of positives' - some £6,250. What Foxen Cooper was proposing, in addition to refixing and rewashing as recommended by Kodak, was the production of 'archive protection masters' printed from the original negatives, an almost unheard of concept. The huge sum of money needed for this may well have provoked some second thoughts over the desirability of trying to preserve old films, but given that there was no one in a position to question Foxen Cooper's recommendations it appears that the go-ahead was given - with the one important proviso that only the more important items were to be given this full conservation treatment.

Choosing the more important items became part of the Museum's first efforts to document its film collection. The task of selection was tackled by the Trustees of the Imperial War Museum (who evidently had considerably more direct involvement with the collections than the Board of Trustees tends to have these days). It is hardly surprising that their priorities differed from those of a later generation. Although a historian of the 1990s would still broadly agree with their selection of the most important films, where they diverged crucially from current thinking was in the way in which they felt films were important: evidently they did not feel that it was of primary concern to preserve complete films intact, as a record not only of events portrayed but also of the editorial policies and artistic judgements of the times. If film was important only for the historical interest of the subject matter, then nothing would be lost - and costs would be saved - if only selected sequences from the films were copied, or if the preserved material did not include the intertitles (the explanatory captions introducing each scene used, before the development of the 'talkies', to convey a film's dialogue or commentary).

Files in the Department of Film testify to an impressive film viewing schedule taken on by the Trustees in the years 1921-1923, although closer examination reveals an embarrassing number of films where there was 'no actual decision received' (including a number of films relating to women in the war, which were viewed exclusively by the Board of Trustees' lady representatives, Lady Norman and Miss Conway), and a great many more films were simply not viewed. Perhaps the Trustees' efforts to produce a comprehensive scene-by-scene breakdown of the entire collection were doomed from the outset. [9]

The approach to film preservation here described, with its emphasis on the selection of important pictures divorced from the context in which they were shown, is alien to much modern thought in the film archive world - not least to the current emphasis on 'restoration' of the work as originally screened as much as on 'preservation' of the material held in the archive. It is in fact so alien that it is perhaps worth stressing that it was not an approach peculiar to the Museum, or confined to the early 1920s. As late as 1955, the historian Sir Arthur Elton wrote that 'the film archive library should have a declared aim on no account to receive more than a

selected minimum. Otherwise, the film archivist will find himself receiving not only the baby but the bath water, the bath, the boiler, the coke bin and the coke'. [10] As for the decision not to preserve the intertitles, Ernest Lindgren, founding curator of the National Film Archive in the 1930s, is known to have felt that newsreel commentaries might be discarded as the pictures were all that counted. [11]

The Museum was not only concerned about saving money by thinking of scrapping the original intertitles. It felt that such captions might be factually inadequate, or embarrassingly propagandist. In its report for 1922-1923, the Museum suggested a scheme to replace the original intertitles.

It has been found that the titles used by the Ministry of Information, while excellent for war propaganda purposes, are useless, and in some cases, misleading as historical records. A new system of titling is being tried in which every section of film will be examined together with the operator's diary and where possible, the war diaries of units engaged, in order to ensure absolute accuracy of description. This work necessarily takes some time ...' [12]

It did indeed require more time than was available and there is - from the restoration point of view, one would have to add, fortunately - no trace of any wholesale retitling in the Museum's film collection as it survives today.

In parallel with the Trustees' consideration, the Museum conducted two other exercises to establish the historical significance of the films, both implied in the paragraph just quoted. One was an attempt systematically to quiz the cameramen who had taken the films about what they had filmed, when and where; the other was a programme of screening the films to panels of military experts. [13] Both exercises proved often to be of only limited value. Subsequent research has led to the conclusion that the cameraman's recollections were not always reliable even about the attribution of particular scenes to particular individuals. As for the expert screenings, rather than producing considered appraisals of the accuracy or value of particular sequences of film, they tended to lead to inaccurate allegations of fakery and a kind of blanket dismissal of the historical value of film which have also been familiar themes in the seventy following years. The poor quality of the results, however, does not diminish the imaginative gesture that the

Museum had made in its attempts to arrive at sound historical appraisal.

While these various selection and appraisal procedures continued, the negative treatment and printing work was begun. In October 1921, a Mr J W Smith, General Manager of the Williamson Film Printing Co, 80-82 Wardour Street, had submitted his tender for the work of refixing and washing of selected negatives (15/- per 100 ft), and subsequent production of 'a soft print on Eastman Rochester No. 1 Positive stock' (at 4d per foot). [14] Mr Smith also came up with a novel suggestion: given that these masters were for long term storage and that film-stock shrinks with age, he advised that the separation of the perforations of the new stock should be some 4% greater than the standard 'to allow for shrinkage in years to come.' Since the typical nitrate film of this vintage has now (in 1994) reached a shrinkage of around 2%, Mr Smith's masters would still be a good 2% over pitch ! Foxen Cooper tactfully turned down this proposal.[15] At the end of the project in 1923 about 80,000 feet of new master positive appears to have been made, a substantial part of the collection in spite of the selection difficulties.

Parallel to the Museum's moves to preserve and document the collection it already had, Major ffoulkes toyed briefly and optimistically with the prospect of continuing the expansion of the archive. In December 1919, he proposed a conference with representatives from the War Office, Admiralty, Air Force, British Museum and Stationery Office (with 'one or two representatives of the Cinematograph trade') to discuss ways by which film records of important national events could continue to be made and preserved. Nothing came of this initiative, which seems to have been an early casualty in a conflict between idealistic ambitions and the realities of available funding. [16]

The Museum did take steps to acquire copies of the newsreel coverage of certain relevant events in the post-war years: for example, film of the ceremonies surrounding the opening of the Museum's exhibitions at the Crystal Palace in 1920 and the return of the Unknown Warrior for burial in Westminster Abbey was acquired in this way, but a suggestion by Foxen Cooper that the Museum arrange its own filming of the unveiling of the Cenotaph was not acted on. [17] Both the Government and the Museum were becoming less than enthusiastic about doing too much to promote the growth of the film collection. The Museum had space and financial problems enough already, and it was not a time when Government cared much for potentially expensive novelties. Film, even as a medium of record, was coming

to be known to fit this category, not least from the Museum's own preservation costings. [18]

One of the films which the Museum failed to acquire was *The National Film* - a classic case history of the different perspectives of those who founded the Museum's film collection and the normally-recognised 'founding' film archivists of the 1930s. *The National Film* would be of enormous interest to film historians today had it survived: it was an epic piece of late-war hate propaganda, depicting the horrors of a German invasion of Britain, made with a huge production budget under the auspices of Lloyd George's National War Aims Committee. The film was scripted by the novelist Hall Caine, directed by the Irish-born Hollywood director Herbert Brenon (whose 'standing among picture people in America rivalled that of Griffith and DeMille') and starred the likes of Ellen Terry, Matheson Lange and Marie Lohr. Unfortunately, dogged by problems including the loss of a first version in a studio fire, the film was not completed until November 1918 by which time events had made it redundant. In 1921, it was being held up to the Parliamentary Committee on Public Accounts as an example of extravagance; a witness was asked if the film would be put in the Imperial War Museum: 'No,' was the reply, 'we have been advised against that as it would merely occupy space.' [19]

Space, in the early years, was at a premium as the Museum lacked a permanent home. While it was temporarily accommodated at Crystal Palace, where a Great War Exhibition was mounted in 1920, Foxen Cooper had to look for appropriate premises - the Crystal Palace itself could only offer ffoulkes use of 'the Polo Stables and also the Iron Building which is situated immediately below the Terrace'. An early suggestion was that negatives be stored at the Howard Hotel, Norfolk Street (then in the hands of the Ministry of Labour and equipped with film storage vaults) but this provided only a partial and temporary solution. The film collection's first permanent home and staff were obtained when 'a small exhibition room and storage vaults' were made available to it at the War Office, and 'a small examining staff was engaged in order that all negatives and positives should be carefully inspected'. [20]

Foxen Cooper was unwilling to give up his ideal that the Museum should take over a much wider responsibility for film in the public sector. From his new base in the War Office, he wrote in 1921: 'It seems desirable in the public interest that a decision should be arrived at with regard to the preservation of Cinematograph Films which, though not directly connected with the War, are undoubtedly of historical interest.'[21] In this he was, however, at odds with the Trustees, as we shall see later. In 1924, Customs and Excise gave notice of their withdrawal of funding from Foxen Cooper's position. For a while the idea was floated that the whole of Foxen Cooper's 'Government' role should be absorbed into the Museum. Unfortunately, the Curator and Trustees were unable to press forward with such radical ideas. While the Museum negotiated its next move - to galleries belonging to the Imperial Institute in South Kensington - it was coming under fire from critics who held that the move, and the Museum itself, were unnecessary extravagances. The Trustees could not add the extra worries and expense of an expanded film role to their problems. [22]

The Treasury instead agreed to a plan to locate Foxen Cooper's post and his section administratively in His Majesty's Stationery Office (HMSO), although they remained geographically housed in the War Office and practically concerned largely with the Museum's collection. Once the Museum had decided it could not absorb the wider role itself, transfer of the Film Section to the Stationery Office made as much sense as any other destination, although the divergence between formal establishment, actual location and major concern helped to foster Foxen Cooper's 'man of mystery' image, as did his splendidly nebulous job title, now formalised as 'Government Cinematograph Advisor'. Foxen Cooper's staff at this time comprised a part-time record keeper, a technician, a messenger (W J Maloney, who became Film Librarian in 1937) and two female assistants.

Lack of space inhibited the Museum's ability to show its films to its visitors. There was no proper public screening room in any of the Museum's homes until the development of the Cinema at Lambeth Road in the late 1960s. Film was, however, represented in the Museum's galleries by several Mutoscope ('What the Butler saw') machines. The Mutoscopes represent the first 'hands-on' audiovisual experience offered to the Museum's visitors - precursors of the interactive videos which formed a prominent part of the launch of the 'New' Imperial War Museum in 1989. The machines operated by showing sequences of still photographs in 'flick book' style. The nine programmes on offer gave access to such famous scenes from the film collection as Allenby's entry into Jerusalem and an 'over the top' scene (presumably the faked one from *Battle of the Somme*); there were also two naval scenes though nothing from the RFC/RAF. As they required the member of the public who wished to view the scene to insert a penny, the Mutoscopes must have been among the Museum's first experiments with

From 1924, 'penny-in-the-slot' Mutoscope viewing machines gave visitors to the galleries in Kensington access to nine famous scenes from the Imperial War Museum film collection. As the original machines wore out, the Museum began to look for replacements like the 'Auto-Movie' machine illustrated. HU65387

attractions that supplemented its revenue. The experiment was a success: by the time of the Museum's report for 1937-1938, when the Director General was describing them as 'worn out' and 'obsolete', he was also noting that they had made a net profit of some £2,700. [23] The Mutoscopes remained in the Museum's stores for many years but were disposed of before the consolidation of storage at Duxford that took place in the 1970s: no trace of them now survives.

Foxen Cooper's role, before and after his formal relocation into HMSO, included supervision of government involvement in film production, both through the release of film from the Museum collection for re-use in new films and in arranging access to government resources by film makers. The commercial exploitation of the films in his care is the one aspect of Foxen Cooper's work on which his more purist successors in the International Federation of Film Archives might be inclined to frown: FIAF stresses the non-commercial role

British solders, hard-pressed in defence of a railway line – from the 1926 feature film *Mons*, made by British Instructional Films with official help organised through Foxen Cooper. FLM 2550

of film archives. His activities in this area were, however, hardly out of control. Although revenue from the re-use of Museum film went to HMSO - the direct linkage between revenue earned and expenditure on preservation to which the Museum has more recently been able to point was not then envisaged - the Museum's Trustees retained the right to grant or refuse permission to use material in compilation films.

They decided almost immediately to keep the cinema trade at arm's length and instructed Foxen Cooper to have nothing to do with approaches from feature film makers. This policy was largely a response to the attempts of a British filmmaker in 1922 to secure actuality footage from the Museum to enhance a film called *How Lord Kitchener Was Betrayed* (first released in 1921) which he had acquired and was re-editing for a new release. Having viewed the film, the Trustees considered it damaging to Lord Kitchener's reputation and decided firmly against giving it any assistance. Their opinion is scarcely surprising: the original film was a melodrama which among other things suggested that Rasputin had betrayed to the Germans the secret of Kitchener's last voyage. The producer (in a letter hoping to forestall any official decision) may have left us a hint of other grounds for displeasure when he sought to reassure the War Office that 'the objectionable female element has now disappeared'. Fearing that Foxen Cooper's commercial zeal might run away with him, the Standing Committee of the Trustees issued a formal instruction to him:

'... without their consent no film or portion of film controlled by the Imperial War Museum should be lent, leased or sold for incorporation in any story, or reconstruction of incidents connected with the war, in which historical events are represented by scenes and actors photographed after the war'. [24]

The decision did not stop the film makers trying, both for archive film and for other services. It is difficult to hold back amused admiration from some of the hopes and expectations that came to the Museum's attention. In 1925, for example, one distributor, importing a filmed version of *The Phantom of the Opera*, had the idea (described by Foxen Cooper as 'as audacious as it is impudent') of laying on a military escort on the docks at Southampton for the arrival of his print ! [25]

One series of films which was almost immediately allowed as an exception to the Trustees' ruling was the sequence of recreations of famous campaigns and battles from the Great War produced at roughly annual intervals through much of the 1920s. These films were made by British Instructional Films and initially released through New Era, which subsequently produced two similar titles of its own. The significant detail here was that the films were made 'by permission of the Army Council' and were thus unlikely to offer the same kind of offence as the Kitchener film. Productions in this series included *The Battle of Jutland* (1921), *Armageddon* (1923 - a reconstruction of the Palestine campaign), *Zeebrugge* (1924), *Ypres* (1925), *Mons* (1926) and *The Battles of the Coronel and Falkland Islands* (1927). New Era, towards the end of the decade, produced *The Somme* (1927) and *Q-Ships* (1928). The series reached a wide audience, and its long run demonstrates its popularity. The two 1927 films achieved the verdict of 'not bad' from the élitist Swiss-based film journal *Close Up* (which 'rarely had a good word to say for a British picture') and earlier films were more enthusiastically received by domestic reviewers. Thus G A Atkinson of the *Sunday Express* said of *Armageddon* 'it uplifts the soul of the nation as no film has ever done' while the *Evening Standard* wrote 'it must be said that this British film production is a work of genius'. Where appropriate, the Museum received a credit ('The Official War Scenes are exhibited by permission of the Trustees of the Imperial War Museum'). [26]

Unfortunately the Museum did not think to require that copies of the British Instructional/New Era films be added to its own collection - as partial reconstructions, they would not have fitted the historical standards that then prevailed. Even within the constraints of historical film, the Trustees were reluctant to extend the collection beyond a narrow interpretation of the Museum's terms of reference. The existence of the

Museum's collection offered the Government an easy way out of occasional potential embarrassments: when the Uruguayan government presented the United Kingdom with film of the funeral of Sir Ernest Shackleton, or when the Treasury found themselves contractually bound to accept a print of a film of a world tour by the Prince of Wales, there was at least an organisation to which the film could be handed. [27] The Trustees did not welcome such unsolicited additions to the collection, and told the Treasury so. They actually gave to the governments of South Africa and Newfoundland films they did not consider of sufficient interest to British posterity. [28] Their failure to be more acquisitive is a source of irritation to their successors now and (to judge from his other activities) was so to Foxen Cooper at the time.

The Museum did arrange the acquisition of some films by programmes of exchange with former allies: the collection includes war films apparently acquired in this way from Belgium and Italy, and also from the USA (although the Film Department's files contain some letters initially declining such an idea.) [29] The Museum was also willing to exchange film with its former enemy. The Treasury raised no objection (although one may detect a mildly truculent reference to the Trustees' earlier expressions of reluctance to expand the collection in a Treasury note observing that 'the advisability of collecting foreign war films in addition to our own does not seem... quite clear'). The Foreign Office, however, at the very highest level pronounced that such dealings with Germany would be 'open to objection'. The initiative came to nothing, again leaving ground for subsequent generations to have to try to make up. [30]

Foxen Cooper himself continued to argue for a more active government role in the filming of important events. He earned himself a flurry of hostile publicity in 1925, when he allocated exclusive rights to the filming of the signing of the Treaty of Locarno to a single newsreel company, Gaumont - a copy of the resulting film survives in the Museum's collection. The hand of frustrated competitors may be suspected in contemporary press stories questioning 'whether so important a matter as the production of history-making films should be practically under the control of any one man'. [31] Foxen Cooper's most conspicuous success in this area came when he was asked to supervise a film for the Foreign Office of the visit to England in 1928 by the King of Afghanistan; while he again made use of a Gaumont cameraman, he was this time careful to make clear that the result was not a Gaumont film. A file on the project which survives in the Museum suggests the many frustrations Foxen Cooper experienced while making this

Some of the passes issued to Foxen Cooper in 1928 when he was commissioned by the Foreign Office to make a film record of the visit to England of the King of Afghanistan. HU 65386

film ('It was with extreme difficulty that I was able to include myself or the operator and his apparatus with the party'), but still remains optimistic that there might be more such films commissioned ('Perhaps the experience gained will be very useful in the future where the Government desires to record a visit of a foreign potentate'). [32] The Foreign Office seems not to have been convinced, and there was no repeat performance.

Even if Foxen Cooper could not always act on his ideas, he continued to air them: an article entitled 'The Museum of the Future - Nucleus of the Collection - Kinema Films and Records' in the *Westminster Gazette* (1 January 1924) is typical of several in which his sentiments may be recognised even though his name is not always given. The most complete development of his arguments is to be found in a lengthy article 'Historical Film Records: The Life of the Nation: A Heritage for Posterity', credited only to 'a Correspondent' but known to be by Foxen Cooper, in *The Times* (19 March 1929). The article uses the preservation of the First World War films as an example of what the nation should be doing:

Works of art and other national treasures have been selected and housed in the public museums and galleries by persons qualified for the task. The selection of films should be carried out with equal care and vision. It should not be left to private societies, but should be undertaken as a national work at the public expense.

Foxen Cooper was still himself concerned with film as historical record, but in the same article also observed

> ...one notes that there has been, as yet, no general desire to preserve for posterity any one of the masterpieces of cinematography, such as *Quo Vadis?* and *Intolerance* .... Perhaps one day some international society with sufficient means at its disposal will form a library of the great films belonging to the various periods since cinematography came into being.'

The creation by the British Film Institute of its 'National Film Library' which would address this gap was still more than five years away.

It has already been seen that the Museum had no facilities to screen film to its visitors. Films could be borrowed for screening outside the Museum, but this does not seem to have been a frequent occurrence. Most of the loans made were granted for purposes of commemoration to British Legion branches and the like. One exception to the pattern occurred in 1927, when the

Cover of the souvenir programme for the premier of the New Era film *The Somme* in 1927, including 'Official War Scenes exhibited by permission of the Trustees of the Imperial War Museum'. HU 65385

proprietor of the Tivoli Theatre hired from the Museum the 1917 film *The Battle of Arras* for his Armistice Day attraction, in competition to the New Era film recreation of *The Somme* which opened in London at the same time. How much of the interest was spontaneous and how much the result of a carefully orchestrated public relations campaign is at this distance impossible to tell, but the screening acquired an astonishing amount of press coverage, some of it favourably comparing the 'real war film' to 'man's puny, uninspired attempts to recreate phases of the late great conflict'. Despite the suggestion that 'part of the film records of the war should be rented to the cinemas every Armistice Week', the Tivoli experiment appears to have been unique. [33]

Usage of the Museum's collection of First World War film in the later part of the inter-war period was hampered by two problems. The first was an increase in costs consequent on technical needs following the cinema trade's switch to sound.

> Before these old 'silent' films can be 'injected' into modern sound productions, producers must go to the expense of 'stretching' them, that is, printing every second picture-frame twice in order to run at the sound film rate of twenty-four pictures per second instead of at the silent film rate of sixteen pictures per second. Producers have also to add sound effects and commentary. [34]

Film companies were willing to go to this extra trouble for as long as popular interest in the subject matter justified it. The second change affecting perception of the Museum's film collection, however, was the increasing anti-war sentiment of the times. Already by the late 1920s there were voices questioning the making of such films as the British Instructional/New Era series - particularly with Government support: it was claimed that 'the British Cinema is Being Used for Militarist Propaganda'. [35] Some of these attacks took care to distinguish between the 'real' war films and the recent productions, but even the Museum's film collection had the problem of intertitles which reflected the chauvinistic attitudes of the times when they were made into a period when the mood of the nation was largely pacifist. Seeking funds from the Treasury in 1933 to print 16mm copies of films for hire, the new Curator L R Bradley noted (at the prompting of Foxen Cooper) that 'the titles were written for purposes of propaganda, and are not at all suitable for present conditions'. A response from Hore-Belisha at the Treasury to Lord Conway, the Museum's Director

General, refused the funds requested for precisely this reason: 'it might be represented as an attempt by the Trustees to "push" war films and thus provoke undesirable political criticism'. [36]

Preservation returned to the top of Foxen Cooper's agenda in the early 1930s. In 1930 he commissioned a report from the Government Chemist, Sir Robert Robinson, on the question of conserving official films. Sir Robert's report is much as one would have expected - he recommended refixing and rewashing, and the production, under rigorous conditions, of new 'soft positive' masters. [37] These new masters, he suggested, might with advantage use 'acetyl cellulose' (cellulose acetate) as the support 'provided that we can satisfy ourselves that it is sufficiently free from brittleness and shrinkage.' In fact, cellulose acetate had been in use as an alternative to cellulose nitrate since the earliest days of the cinema, particularly for amateur films, as it did not suffer from the dangerous inflammability of the latter. It did, however, have a reputation for brittleness, shrinking and a degree of chemical instability.

Armed with Sir Robert's report, the Museum managed once more to persuade the Treasury to provide the funding necessary to produce over the next two or three years a large number of archive masters on an acetate filmstock which had been specifically manufactured by Kodak. Once again, only selected portions of the films were copied, the bulk of which were those that had already been preserved some ten years earlier on nitrate film. The resulting masters are remarkable for their apparent freedom from the usual ills afflicting early 'safety' film - they are not particularly shrunk or brittle, and show no sign of the chemical decomposition which can affect acetate film of much more recent vintage.

Another renewal of activity in the 1930s involved the documentation of the collection - the 'messenger' Maloney was given the task of producing shotlists and indexes for all the films, and the results of his labours (commenced in 1934) remained the basic route for access into the original First World War collection until it was extensively re-catalogued in the 1980s by Stephen Badsey. [38] Maloney's new duties justified his formal 'establishment' in the Civil Service, and he would be appointed Film Librarian in 1937.

This renewal of effort in the important archival areas of preservation and documentation of the Imperial War Museum film archive is the last major landmark in Foxen Cooper's career: he died in May 1934. His reputation as a man of mystery was evident in his obituaries. *Kinematograph Weekly* wrote 'So quiet and unostentatious in his manner was E. Foxen Cooper ... that there are many in the industry who hardly knew his name .... He was to be seen at important film functions, where he was observant rather than communicative, but when applied to for advice or information was courteous and business like' [39]. When Major ffoulkes retired from the Imperial War Museum a year earlier, he wrote in a farewell letter to Foxen Cooper:

> I should like to thank you very sincerely for all your help and advice in the Cinematograph Section. As you may remember, we began under very difficult conditions, when the cinematograph was not treated seriously by the powers that be, and we had an uphill fight to make them recognise the importance of the war films as historic records. In this your knowledge and experience was of the very greatest assistance and I shall always look back on our collaboration with very great pleasure.' [40]

Although it was still not over when ffoulkes and Foxen Cooper left the scene, the uphill fight has ultimately been a successful one. The film archive of the Imperial War Museum, with further growth after the Second World War, now holds some 70 million feet of film, and is an internationally-recognised source for the filmed history of the twentieth century. Its origins, however, are clearly to be traced in the period 1919-1934. It is both salutary and amusing to note how many of the issues important to film archivists in the 1990s had been explored in these fifteen years, before the concept of the film archive had any currency. If the exploration had sometimes led to dead ends, and if Foxen Cooper and his successors were turned back from some of the more inviting goals by lack of resources, it does not diminish the power of his extraordinary vision. He was clearly a remarkable man, and deserves more widespread recognition.

Notes

1. This expression comes from an undated 1930s draft 'Report on the Work of the Government Cinematograph Adviser' which notes, it must be said, that the days of such opinions 'have vanished'. This draft is one of several papers from the inter-war period held in the Imperial War Museum's Department of Film, hereafter abbreviated in these notes to IWM(Film). Other sources consulted in the preparation of this article are the Museum's central files, hereafter IWM(CF), the Museum's press cuttings albums, and files in the Public Record Office, Kew.

2. Minutes of the Imperial War Museum Board of Trustees; first meeting, 10 December 1920, IWM(CF).

3. An extremely readable history of film archives is provided in *Keepers of the Frame* by Penelope Houston, British Film Institute 1994. The rules quoted are listed in the FIAF Statutes, 1993 edition, p 2.

4. Foxen Cooper's record card is preserved in the Greater London Record Office (Modern Records); quotations are from the London *Evening News*, 12 May 1934, and *Evening Standard*, 2 December 1925; details of his secondment to Customs and Excise etc are in the Public Record Office, Kew (hereafter PRO) in STAT 14/438, Foxen Cooper to Controller HMSO, 22 September 1924, and the exchange of letters between the Museum and the Treasury (October/November 1920) is in IWM(Film).

5. Report by Messrs Kodak on the Preservation of Cinematograph Films, 1920, IWM(Film).

6. Experience now shows that it is the instability of cellulose nitrate, the plastic used in the manufacture of most professional films up to 1950, which normally dictates the lifetime of a film, rather than any fading of the photographic image through inadequate washing and fixing.

7. Foxen Cooper to ffoulkes, 28 September 1920, IWM(Film).

8. Extract from 'Report on the Preservation of Official War Films - Estimates', 2 October 1920, IWM(Film). The Museum's total estimate bid for Financial Year 1921-1922 was £39,900 so the intended commitment to film preservation by the infant Museum amounted to 15% of its budget, IWM(CF).

9. 'List No. 1: Films Already Seen by Trustees of the Imperial War Museum', 'List No. 2: Films Not Yet Seen by Trustees of the Imperial War Museum' etc, IWM(Film). The lists contain summaries of the films viewed, the viewing dates, and the decisions and actions taken.

10. Sir Arthur Elton, 'The Film as Source Material for History' in *Aslib Proceedings* Vol 7, No 4 (November 1955), quoted in Penelope Houston, *op cit*, p 114. Modern film archivists, of course, still recognise this dilemma, while tending to wish that they, not their predecessors, had made the selection.

11. Penelope Houston, *op cit*, p 43.

12. Imperial War Museum, *6th Annual Report (3rd Report of the Board of Trustees)* 1922-1923, p 16.

13. Evidence of the former activity includes F W Engholm to Foxen Cooper, 30 January 1925, replying to 'your request in the Kinematograph Weekly of January 22nd, 1925' with a listing of the films for which Engholm had been responsible, IWM(Film). Examples of the latter exercise - also IWM(Film) - include a note entitled 'Particulars of "Battle of Somme" film screened on 4 May 1922 before Imperial War Museum Trustees and comments thereon by technical officers of the Navy and Army'.

14. J W Smith to Foxen Cooper, 27 October 1921, IWM(Film). The same address was subsequently Studio Film Laboratories Ltd, now Soho Images Ltd. A 'soft print' or 'soft positive' was a low-contrast master copy from which duplicate negatives could in turn be struck.

15. Foxen Cooper to J W Smith, 1 November 1921, IWM(Film).

16. Letter from ffoulkes to Burke, 1 December 1919, IWM(Film).

17. Correspondence between Gaumont and Imperial War Museum, October-November 1920, and between Pathé Frères and Imperial War Museum, November-December 1920; Foxen Cooper to ffoulkes, 5 November 1920, IWM(Film).

18. PRO FO 395-329: Treasury to FO, 12 March 1920: 'expenditure for this purpose [*ie* film propaganda] should be greatly curtailed in the coming year and should cease at the earliest date possible.'

19. Nicholas Reeves, *Official British Film Propaganda during the First World War*, Croom Helm 1986, pp 125-130; Kevin Brownlow, *The War, the West and the Wilderness*, Secker & Warburg 1979, pp 156-158; 'Half-a-ton of War Film - Propaganda Picture that Came Too Late' in *Northern Echo*, 20 January 1921.

20. Correspondence between the Museum, the Crystal Palace Trustees, the Treasury, the War Office, the Foreign Office, the Office of Works, etc 1920-1923 in IWM(Film); the final two quotations are from *Report of the Imperial War Museum 1920-21*, uncorrected proof copy in IWM(CF), p 37.

21. Foxen Cooper to ffoulkes, 28 April 1921, IWM(Film).

22. File A4/4 Treasury Cinematograph, IWM(CF).

23. File 'Mutascopes [sic] and other automatic viewing machines 1923-38', IWM(Film); Imperial War Museum, *20th Annual Report of the Director General to the Board of Trustees 1937-1938*, HMSO 1938, p 14.

24. Rachael Low, *The History of the British Film 1918-1929*, Alln & Unwin 1971 (p 138); Arthur Freeman to War Office, 17 January 1922, IWM(Film); Minutes of the Thirteenth Meeting of the Standing Committee, 15 March 1922, IWM(CF).

25. Correspondence between Foxen Cooper, European Motion Picture Co Ltd, the War Office etc, June 1925, IWM(Film).

26. Rachael Low, *op cit*, pp 22 and 181; *Sunday Express*, 11 November 1923; *Evening Standard*, 13 November 1923; Souvenir programme from the premier of *The Somme*, IWM(Film).

27. PRO FO 371-8529: 'Request by Curator of Imperial War Museum for film of funeral of Sir E. Shackleton.'

28. '... the Trustees were strongly of opinion that no films should be accepted by this Department except those of actual war interest, or recording conditions at home or overseas directly connected with the War': ffoulkes to Treasury, 3 February 1921; correspondence between ffoulkes and Treasury, November 1923, File A4/4 Treasury Cinematograph, IWM(CF).

29. *A la Gloire du Troupier Belge/Ter Eere van den Belgischen Soldat* Parts 1-5 (in the film collection as IWM 1050-1054); *Amid Snow and Ice on Mount Tonale* and *The Other Italian Army* (IWM 459-460); *Pictorial History of the War* Nos 1-14 (IWM 501/01-14).

30. Correspondence between ffoulkes, the Treasury and the Foreign Office on File A4/4 Treasury Cinematograph, IWM(CF). The Museum initiated a programme of exchanges with film archives in (then) both East and West Germany in the 1980s.

31. *Gaumont Graphic 1534* and 2 reels of associated unedited material are in the film collection as IWM 810 and 811; press stories included 'Whitehall's Film Controller', *Evening Standard*, 2 December 1925, and 'Autocrat of the Films', *Daily Express*, 4 December 1925 - the quoted comment comes from the former.

32. *Visit of the King of Afghanistan to England*, in the film collection as IWM 809; file 'References to filming of H.M. Amir of Afghanistan visit. March 1928.' IWM(Film).

33. 'Real War Film', *Star*, 12 November 1927.

34. *Imperial War Museum, 18th Annual Report of the Director-General and of the Curator and Secretary to the Board of Trustees, 1934-1935*, HMSO 1935. The use of stretch printing to prevent the caricature appearance of silent film used at the wrong speed was one of the features of the BBC's series *The Great War* in the 1960s, some of the publicity for which suggested it was a new technique.

35. 'War on the War Film ... by Lt.-Commander the Hon. J.M. Kenworthy, R.N., M.P.', *Reynolds News*, 20 November 1927.

36. Foxen Cooper to Bradley, 10 November 1933; Bradley to Treasury, 6 March 1934; Hore-Belisha to Conway, 21 June 1934, IWM(Film).

37. Report on the Examination of War Films, Government Laboratory, 23 May 1930, IWM(Film).

38. The results of Stephen Badsey's work will be published as *The Imperial War Museum Film Catalogue Volume 1: the First World War Archive* by Flicks Books in November 1994.

39. *Kinematograph Weekly*, 17 May 1934, p4. The Museum's own press cuttings album contains only one notice of Foxen Cooper's death, from the *Evening News*, 12 May 1934. Headlined 'The London Fireman Who Became The Government's Own Film Man ... A Whitehall Man of Mystery Dead', it consists largely of material used in the Locarno Treaty story nine years earlier, but does mention the 'official war films' and Foxen Cooper's work for their 'preservation and cataloguing'.

40. ffoulkes to Foxen Cooper, 12 June 1933, IWM(Film).

Acknowledgments

The photograph of Edward Foxen Cooper is reproduced by courtesy of the British Newspaper Library, Colindale. The authors of this article acknowledge the earlier work done by Clive Coultass and Anne Fleming, former Keepers of the Department of Film, in researching the Department's history, and the assistance of Suzanne Bardgett whose reminder of the existence of the Museum's press cuttings albums opened up an important source of information.

Film as Allied assistance: Captain Bromhead's mission to Russia, 1916-1917

Kay Gladstone

Kay Gladstone is Acquisitions and Documentation Officer in the Department of Film.

On February 4th 1916, Alfred Bromhead, a captain in the British Army, arrived in Petrograd at the start of an official mission to show Russian audiences films demonstrating 'England's present efforts towards the achievement of victory'. [1] His mission, covertly sponsored by the Foreign Office, would last until September 1917. The visit has a special importance in the history of British film propaganda since Bromhead's tool of persuasion was *Britain Prepared*, a documentary compilation and the first film specifically made to influence foreign opinion in neutral and allied countries.

This article will sketch the political background to Bromhead's assignment and describe the practical aspects of his work in Russia, relying mainly but not exclusively on his own edited Diary and official reports based on this unpublished source. [2] Since it is never easy to assess the impact of film propaganda separately from the effect on morale of such other influences as newspapers, military reverse, revolution and hunger, Bromhead's actual influence in Russia cannot, in the absence of corroborating evidence, be exactly defined. More easily assessed is the official perception of his influence, so favourable that it did much to confirm British belief in the importance of overseas film propaganda for the remainder of the First World War and the duration of the Second.

The Background

The secret section of the Foreign Office responsible for generating and disseminating British propaganda in 1915 to neutral and allied countries was located at Wellington House in Buckingham Gate, London. Wellington House officials believed that since the outbreak of war 'the German Bureaux have been using on a large scale the cinematographs of neutral countries', and gave credit to the Germans for having 'rightly recognised that the cinematograph forms a kind of "Bible" to the working people in many countries where newspapers and books and pamphlets would never reach them'. [3] It is debatable how far this early admiration for German film propaganda was justified (some Germans actually considered that their own efforts in this area lagged behind the achievements of the Allies). [4] More significant was the competitive spirit which it prompted, as a result of which the Foreign Office, after a year's struggle with the security-obsessed War Office and Admiralty, succeeded in obtaining pictures of the Grand Fleet in the North Sea, the build-up of Britain's New

61

Armies and the making of munitions by Vickers. Drawing on this, together with Vickers' own record and promotional material, *Britain Prepared – A Review of the Activities of His Majesty's Naval and Military Forces*, was rapidly assembled and premiered in London in December 1915. [5]

The prosaic title is a fair reflection of the factual content: the film inter-titles name no enemy and do not pretend that training scenes are operational activities; in content, style and emotion the film is far removed from the second major British documentary compilation of the war, *The Battle of the Somme,* (August 1916) sponsored by the War Office and widely distributed by the Foreign Office in neutral and allied countries.

By the start of 1916 Wellington House was therefore in a position to test the validity of its own earlier findings 'that there is a great demand for such pictures in probably all neutral and allied countries'. [6] 'The same report referred to 'an undercurrent of uneasiness ... in Russia, as to whether the efforts and sacrifices being made by England were comparable with those of our Allies or commensurate with the importance of the struggle' and foresaw 'a very great development of propagandism in Russia' in the near future. [7] This quickening realisation of the potential of film to influence events at a crucial juncture of the war explains why within ten days of the London première of *Britain Prepared* the Foreign Office was ready to send the film to Petrograd.

Captain Alfred Bromhead

The person selected to take the film was Captain Alfred Claude Bromhead, co-founder in 1898 with Thomas Welsh (one of the four members of the Wellington House Cinema Committee) of the Gaumont Company in Britain. The business had been set up as a branch of the French concern, initially to sell imported equipment and films, although Gaumont films were soon produced in Britain and the English office, in Cecil Court, off the Charing Cross Road, later became one of the most important selling agents in the world for both British and foreign films. [8]

As a pioneer British film executive who had personal experience of production, distribution and exhibition, Bromhead appeared a good choice. He had witnessed the transition from fair-ground screenings of films to their exhibition in specially constructed picture palaces such as he had himself built in Bishopsgate in 1904. [9] His seven years' experience in the British Volunteers (1900-1907) [10] was an advantage, for it was expected that his uniform would greatly assist him in obtaining facilities in Russia. [11] His fluent French was a further asset, for the language was widely spoken in the Russian court and by many of the Army officers he would meet.

Arrival in Petrograd

Bromhead's first tasks on arrival in Petrograd were to report to the British Ambassador, Sir George Buchanan, who had assumed Wellington House's earlier responsibility for propaganda in Russia, and to meet the Gaumont Company's representatives in Petrograd and Moscow, Monsieur Kapelli and Monsieur Chassaign. These initial meetings on the same day (5 February 1916) hint at the ambivalent nature of Bromhead's mission from the outset, for he had been asked by Wellington House to arrange, on the one hand, for the commercial screening of the film throughout Russia via the agency of the Gaumont Company and, on the other hand, to endeavour to make arrangements through Buchanan for a special inaugural performance in the presence of Tsar Nicholas II. [12] This would be an essential prelude to gaining permission to show the film to the soldiers in the rest camps behind the fighting lines.

Wellington House initially attached much importance to the commercial distribution of the film, as may be inferred from their earlier choice of Léon Gaumont, head of the French parent company, to carry out the mission to Russia. Reliance on a multi-national company (which advertised itself on its English letterhead as 'Contractors to the British and French Governments') may have represented a realistic approach to the Russian film market, dominated since its birth by the rival French companies of Pathé and Gaumont, but Wellington House's confidence in the marketability of its product quickly proved to be misplaced.

Buchanan had already reported to the Foreign Office that 'the programmes of most cinema theatres here generally consist of a drama, a comedy and films representing more important recent events. Amongst last named have appeared pictures of our troops training on Salisbury Plain or marching through London but they have not interested the public. What would be really attractive would be pictures of our Navy and battle scenes.' [13]

Far from considering the film's inadequacies from a foreign audience's point of view, Wellington House made no attempt to accede to Buchanan's requests. They had anticipated showing the film as a whole, lasting two and a half hours, in larger towns, and in smaller towns dividing the programme into two parts, military and naval. [14] Their inexpert handling of *Britain*

Prepared is understandable: this may not be surprising given that the propagandists in London were mostly writers who were more familiar with shaping text into articles and books than with editing the new and unfamiliar propaganda medium of film.

The reaction at the Embassy to the private screening of *Britain Prepared* was disappointment that no battle scenes had been included and a firm view that the film was too long. The Gaumont representative and the Embassy concurred that the film's commercial prospects were 'distinctly discouraging'. There was neither sufficient 'sensation' nor incident of direct Russian interest to appeal to the general public. [15]

There was indeed a wide choice of film entertainment available to the general public in Russia in 1916. One hundred and sixty-four production and distribution firms were in existence, thirty of which were actively engaged in making new films, ranging from an adaptation from Pushkin of *The Queen of Spades* to such lurid titles as *The Wolf of Moscow, Thirsty for Love* and *In the Claws of the Yellow Devil*. [16] The atmosphere in which such popular melodramas were shown was well caught by the novelist Hugh Walpole, who as head of the Anglo-Russian Commission in Petrograd oversaw all forms of British propaganda to Russia:

> The cinema door blazed with light, and around it was gathered a group of soldiers and women and children, peering in at a soldiers' band, which, placed on benches in a corner of the room, played away for its very life. Outside around the door were large bills announcing *The Woman Without a Soul, Drama in four parts,* and there were fine pictures of women falling over precipices, men shot in bedrooms, and parties in which all the guests shrank back in extreme horror from the heroine. We went inside and were overwhelmed by the band, so that we could not hear one another speak. The floor was covered with sunflower seeds, and there was a strong smell of soldiers' boots and bad cigarettes and urine. We bought tickets from an old Jewess behind the pigeon-hole and then, pushing the curtain aside, stumbled in. Here the smell was different, being, quite simply that of human flesh not very carefully washed ...

> No one could have denied that it was a cheerful scene. Soldiers, sailors, peasants,

> women and children crowded together upon the narrow benches... There was a tremendous amount of noise. Mingled with the strains of the band beyond the curtain were cries and calls and loud roars of laughter. The soldiers embraced the girls...

> The lights were down and we were shown pictures of Paris. Because the cinema was a little one and the prices were small the films were faded and torn... There were comments all round the room in exactly the spirit of children before a conjuror at a party... (from *The Secret City*) [17]

To his colleague in the London office of Gaumont Bromhead confided 'You must abandon all idea that there is a profit to be made'. [18] The film's exposure in Russia would now be almost wholly dependent on the Ambassador obtaining from the Tsar an order that the film be shown to his soldiers at the front.

Bromhead spent the next few weeks reducing the length of the film to about 6000ft (100 minutes), removing all repetitions, 'rearranging' and fixing in translated titles, and, under the guidance of the Ambassador's Private Secretary, H J Bruce, preparing for the special inaugural performance in the presence of the Tsar. [19] (These and other references to the cutting and preparation of 'the short set of films' (10 March 1916) and later 'two long reels' (7 April 1916) remain tantalising details for the historian since nowhere does this propagandist indicate what parts he adapted for his various audiences, nor why.)

Screening of *Britain Prepared* before the Tsar

Approval for Bromhead to tour the Russian fronts with *Britain Prepared* could not be given until the Tsar had viewed a version of the film. The Tsar's interest in films was not new, the court having had its own official cameraman (Kurt von Hahn-Tagielski) since 1900, and the Tsar once a week customarily describing to the Tsarina his visit to the cinema – 'no matter through what crisis Russia or the Russian Army was passing'. [20] Bromhead himself noted how command cinema performances were held every week to see the latest films, 'chiefly French and Italian drama'. (10/10/16) The cinema was a shared entertainment for the Imperial family. The Tsarevich had even been presented with a projector and films by the Pathé Company, [21] his English tutor Charles Sydney Gibbes noting on separate occasions in his diary what his charge saw at the kinematograph:

'two new episodes from *The Mysterious Hand of New York* – 28/11/1916'; 'Saw war pictures, two episodes from *The Mysterious Hand*, and one comic – 9/1/1917.' [22]

Bromhead was well satisfied by the Imperial première, held in the private theatre of the Palace at Tsarskoye Selo on 5th March 1916:

> Show went off fine – no hitches. Congratulated by Tsar who shook hands with me twice – also Tsarina and Tsarevich – omitted to kiss Queen's hand. Tsar promised to see films again at front and to arrange for me to go there shortly ... Tsarevich came into operating chamber [projection area] – very nice boy.

The Tsar was present when a second screening took place on 24th March at the Stavka or Army GHQ at Mogilev, this time in the presence of about twenty five people including the Grand Dukes and the head of the British Military Mission, General Hanbury Williams. This too was a 'complete success', the Tsar giving orders that his staff were to arrange for Bromhead to visit all fronts. The Tsar's private reaction to this particular film is not known but may possibly be inferred from his enthusiastic but uncritical comments on other screenings of Allied material: 'We were shown part of a very interesting English military film ... remarkably interesting and entertaining.'; about Verdun 'saw an interesting French picture at the cinematograph'. [23] This mention of French film echoes oblique references in Bromhead's Diary at this period to competition with French film propaganda in Russia. 'HE, ie Buchanan, doing his damnedest to keep French films out of Mariinsky' 4/4/16. The Foreign Office propagandists were evidently concerned lest French influence predominate over British efforts to impress their Russian ally, the covert eventual aim being the prospect of commercial advantage in Russia after the end of the war.

Another contemporary reaction to *Britain Prepared* comes from the Chief of the British Naval Mission to Russia (1915-16), Rear-Admiral Richard Phillimore, in a letter to his wife on 29th March 1916:

> 'Yesterday I saw the official British Cinematograph, which is being sent round to let the Russians know what the British Army and Navy are doing. It was rather good, especially the naval part ... This is the 5th performance in this little town and was for girls' schools ...' [24]

The little town was actually Mogilev, where Phillimore and his Army counterpart were in close contact with the Tsar, another reminder that Bromhead's film mission was just one aspect of a wider British (and Allied) service presence in Russia to support her wavering morale and faltering military might.

Promotion of *Britain Prepared*

Now that the film had received the all-important blessing of the Tsar, Bromhead was able to devote most of April 1916 to trying to promote the film by press and official shows in Petrograd, and arranging for its commercial release in the city and elsewhere (two prints of the film were sold outright to a Siberian buyer, Bromhead having previously established that the notion of copyright in film was to all practical purposes ignored in Russia). [25] His Diary entries for this month show how he did all within his power, as a British Army junior officer but highly experienced cinema showman, to ensure the successful launch of the film:

> Arrived Mariinsky 8 p.m. – watched show from behind – very nervous of fire, great risk and near thing. Light splendid and show a great success. Everything 100 p.c. – better than yesterday. Saw Ambassador and Attaché – warmly congratulated on show. Front seat in centre reserved for me – magnificent scene – uniforms, etc. Emperor not there. (7/4/16)

One press review of the film was so complimentary that it might almost have been written by Bromhead himself, who immediately forwarded it to London:

> Yesterday I went to England for three hours! It cost me 5 kopecks on tram No. 9. And yet there are people who abuse the cinematograph! Yesterday at any rate the cinema rose to the occasion, and I am very grateful to it. It made it possible for me to peep as it were through a chink in the wall and see what is being done in England – what a colossal effort is being made by our loyal ally ... For us civilians there was a lesson to be learnt. Even in that conventional presentation (the cinema is not always wholly truthful) we felt the concentrated cheerfulness of a nation, alien to war by its very nature, but plunging as one man into hard collective toil. What impressed me most of all was the mobilisation of industry. There was something to envy ...

But there's no telling all we saw ... This gigantic effort cannot fail to inspire in us cheerfulness and confidence in ourselves. (6 April 1916) [26]

A fortnight later a series of three shows on the same day to a total audience of 6,000 soldiers satisfied Bromhead the impresario less: 'Poor show and bad waits [between reel changes] – Young Ivan only translating'. (20/4/16)

A 'slight fire' eight days later proved that Bromhead's earlier fears of a conflagration of inflammable nitrate film in the Mariinsky Theatre were well founded, and also perhaps cast doubt (shortly to be justified) on the reliability of his locally engaged Russian projectionist, on whose skills the forthcoming tour would so much depend.

First screening tour: The Ukraine

The first screening tour, to the Southern Front of General Brusilov, began on 15 May. With his British orderly Private Greengrass and 'George' Gregoriev, together with five large cases of cinema appliances, Bromhead set off by train from Petrograd to Kiev and the Ukraine. After arranging for several matinée screenings in theatres to audiences ranging from schoolchildren to wounded soldiers and the local Army commanders Generals Brusilov and Diederichs, which generally took place in the afternoon, Bromhead arranged the first of the many open-air night-time shows which became a feature of this and subsequent tours.

The Diary evokes the atmosphere of a screening to the Minsk Regiment:

Toasts as usual then back to staff where open air show great success – could have had double the men – Gregoriev a great worry – got the wrong idea. Basilovitch [Russian Conducting Officer] speaks of it. Wonderful scene – guns booming – moonlight – bands playing and films working – General calls for three cheers for England. Supped with Generals afterwards. More champagne. Home by car at midnight. (14/5/16)

Proximity to the front not only provided the authenticity of live sound effects but also gave easy access to a dynamo, borrowed from a searchlight outfit for the purpose of supplying light to the projector. It was indeed General Brusilov's inability to spare searchlight dynamos once operations recommenced which brought Bromhead's first tour to a close on 19 June 1916.

These open air screenings appear to have been rousing performances, accompanied on at least one occasion by a band playing 'God Save the King' during the march-past sequence in the film and often concluded by patriotic speeches on the theme of the comradeship-in-arms between the Russian and British soldiers, and toasts which Bromhead would answer in English or French. Bromhead's major handicap on this tour was however not his elementary level of Russian (he had started lessons upon arrival in Petrograd) but the unreliability and laziness of his closest Russian comrade-in-arms, Gregoriev the projectionist.

Upon his return to Petrograd Bromhead evaluated the success of his tour in two Reports (Nos 7 and 8) to Wellington House. He estimated that his total of forty four shows (ranging from performances in small and suffocating theatres seating a few hundred to an open air show with an audience of 9,000 at Ratchisai) had been seen by approximately 100,000 soldiers and 3,000 officers. The open air shows, he considered, were by far the most satisfactory.

Many thousand men can at one time see the films at any hour after dark; and provided the weather is fine, which so far has generally been the case, the conditions for all concerned are easier and pleasanter.

There was the additional advantage of flexibility, enabling 'the picture to be brought to any spot, even close to the trenches'. Indeed in some places eight men from each company in the frontlines themselves were recalled from the trenches.

The men were fully armed, ready to leave at a moment's notice in case of alarm, rifles being piled during the show and the men seated on the ground.

Another interesting aspect of the open air shows, sketched diagramatically by Bromhead, was that the audience was seated on both sides of the screen, with the Generals and Staff and some troops in the front rows on the side of the projector and dynamo, while the rest of the troops on the other side of the screen watched the action in reverse, seeing British soldiers apparently saluting with the left hand.

During the shows Bromhead sat with the commanding general and other officers, briefly commenting on the films shown or answering questions about Britain's forces to the best of his ability. He was assisted in his ambassadorial role by Private Greengrass, whose contact with the soldiers later made him fluent in Russian and who on one occasion was presented by a General to his troops 'as a specimen of the British soldier … his men were very anxious to see what a British soldier was like'. Bromhead was aware, however, that not only were both he and Greengrass unfamiliar with conditions on the Western Front (the first dead German soldier he had seen had been in Russia), but that his film, made in 1915, failed to give a picture of current events in France.

In another respect, however, Bromhead was fully up to date. His first-hand acquaintance with the Army on the Southern Front probably placed him in a better position than the diplomats and officers in Petrograd and Mogilev to comment on the morale of the Russian forces:

> Russian sentiment towards England in this war appears to consist chiefly of hopeful expectancy. They feel keenly that they have themselves made immense sacrifices and efforts. Many think that they have done and are doing more than the other allies, but they lack self-confidence and certainly do not feel strong to win alone.

On the reception of the film, Bromhead was more guarded:

> …the men much appreciated the shows and were particularly interested in the scenes from the front and the navy. Naturally, for troops who had been in the field for many months pictures of merely training in England were not so interesting. [27]

Commercial screening of *Britain Prepared*

Back in Petrograd, while waiting to receive orders from the Russian GHQ to tour another front, Bromhead discovered how *Britain Prepared* had fared commercially. Although twelve of the sixteen copies had found distributors, the only precise figures available to Bromhead from the Gaumont representative were based on the three-week booking of the film at the Parisiana Theatre in Petrograd, and there only the first week had been profitable. This confirmed the Russian cinema trade's negative predictions, but Bromhead deftly converted this disappointing news into a positive statement to the Petrograd and provincial press that 'Russian War Charities have benefitted considerably by various exhibitions which have been given in Petrograd of

the British cinema films depicting England's efforts and preparations in the Great War'. [28] The sum of 831.60 roubles (£55) was duly paid to a selection of charities chosen by Lady Buchanan.

Second screening tour: Finland

Bromhead's next tour was to the Grand Duchy of Finland and lasted from 18 July to 14 August. His Diary entries and Tenth Report reveal entirely different conditions from those encountered in the Ukraine. Nearly all the fifty three shows to an estimated audience of 37,000 were given in proper cinemas, although in one town (Viborg) the Finnish proprietor of the only available theatre initially declined to lend or hire his premises. Bromhead, touring from one Russian garrison to another, was otherwise insulated from the pro-German sympathies of the educated Finns, but he did note that 'Finland, generally speaking, is neither friendly to Russia nor to her Allies'.

He again found that just as important as screening films on the tour was the opportunity that personal contact gave him to reassure his hosts of the friendly feelings the British Army and people had towards Russia, for this 'is the sort of thing that cannot be told too often to the Russians, as it heartens them and they have a tendency to be easily disheartened'. [29]

Anxieties about film propaganda in Russia

'Went Kapelli – Mil Mission about new moves. Much worried and depressed all day – wrote Chassaign about films for Helsingfors – started report'. (15/8/16)

This uncharacteristically disheartened Diary entry and other references following his return to

Captain Bromhead stands flanked by Russian officers of 421 Tsarskoye Selo Regiment and Raumo Garrison, Finland, 21 July 1916. Q114368

Petrograd indicate that Bromhead may have been caught up at this point in wranglings between the Foreign Office and the War Office. Certainly Bromhead's enlistment of the support of Major Sir Samuel Hoare of the British Military Mission to press for a 'new set of films' (17/8/16) provoked indignation in Wellington House at the prospect of a representative of the War Office interfering in propaganda matters outside his competence.

In his Tenth Report to Wellington House Bromhead expressed the view that 'the film is now nearly played out and should be replaced by an entirely new and very carefully arranged film, to consist of views from the front and certain features which do not appear in the present series, much, I think, to its disadvantage'. He also voiced concern that the prior commercial screening of *Britain Prepared* would preempt and spoil the impact of his own screenings, although he pointedly conceded that in the present situation where his films were more than six months old 'it is not advisable to handicap the commercial exploitation further'. It would appear that Bromhead, who had single-handedly initiated the distribution of British film propaganda in Russia, was no longer to enjoy paramount local control.

A series of war films had indeed already been sent in early June via Wellington House 'not to Bromhead, who said that he could not deal with any more' but directly to the Gaumont representative in Russia to handle on commercial lines. [30] By September Wellington House had however broken the link with Bromhead's earlier company and was in negotiations with 'a new and promising concessionaire who we think will do better than Gaumont'. [31]

The Battle of the Somme

The subject of those negotiations was *The Battle of the Somme*, first shown to an invited audience in London on 10th August and sent to the Embassy in Petrograd in early September. Bromhead was able to view a copy on 17 September immediately after his return to Petrograd from his third screening tour, this time to the Northern Front (28 August – 16 September).(During one evening show in Riga (5/9/16) the customary cheers and band music had been held in check as in the darkness a German Zeppelin passed overhead. Later during supper, its bombs were heard to drop, fortunately some way off.)

Bromhead was well pleased by this long battle film, writing directly to Gowers that 'it is certainly very fine and is quite the sort of thing I want for the soldiers at the front. The artillery work is grand in this film and will much hearten the Russians'.

The same letter indicated what topics Bromhead believed should be included in British propaganda films for 'great practical profit to the Russians, and increased prestige for the British. Such as trench appliances and their uses – (Sniperscopes – trench guns and general trench equipment where it varies from the Russian practice). Machine guns – emplacements and tactics illustrated – Sisters – Nurses and Ambulance or Hospital Work. Gassing drill tactics. Flame projectors ditto – and twenty other things I could mention. Not forgetting ever a humorous element as the Russian soldier wants something to laugh at.' [32]

The Battle of the Somme now had to be launched both officially and commercially. Although not responsible for the film's general distribution, Bromhead was nevertheless keen to supervise the editing and translation of the concessionaire's explanatory titles for the film 'in the British interest'. [33] Arrangements were also made for the Tsar to see the film at Mogilev, another Imperial première vividly described in the Diary: Captain Bromhead had on this occasion first to overcome the interference of a Russian general who had decided without consultation that only two of the film's five reels would be shown to the Tsar, to allow 'a drama, rotten one at that' to be shown in place of the 'fine war pictures'.

> Stand round room as usual – Tsar comes round. General Waters presents me – Tsar says he remembers me well and asks if I will show him films. I say, I understand I am only to show a small part and not the most interesting. Tsar says, Why? Are they too long?. I say, no – under an hour. General Waters intervenes, No, Your Majesty – General Kondorovski has decided that you are not to be allowed to see them because of the Tsarevich and the actual dead to be seen – Tsar, but I want to see them all, we will see about it. General Waters, see the General again and arrange it between you. (10/10/16)

In the event the Tsar and his son saw the first two reels on the 10th and the last three reels two nights later, together with one Vickers film on the manufacturing of big cannon. Bromhead noted in his Diary 'Deep impression made on all present', (12/10/16) but probably more striking to the modern day film goer is this evidence that complete films at this early stage of cinema history were shown episodically without even arousing comment.

Fourth screening tour: The Caucasus

Bromhead now set off on his fourth screening tour, to the Caucasus Front (31 October – 24 December), just after attending a disastrous press show for *The Battle of the Somme* at which only three journalists were present. The late dispatch of invitations was blamed, but whatever the real cause the contrast with the earlier French screening in Moscow of their own Somme film, complete with a claque shouting 'Vive la France' and 'Vive la Russie' at appropriate moments, must have placed the British film at a disadvantage. The pervasive influence of the French was also evident to Bromhead in Tiflis where he learnt that a French captain was in Georgia too, touring with films, presumably in competition with the British.

The Grand Duke Nicholas's wife and daughter expressed their reactions to the scenes of dead and wounded in the film which Bromhead showed them at the Palace (13/11/16): she shared the opinion of the Grand Duke that the films must have been taken under difficult conditions, and were 'quite a historical record', while Princess Tatiana responded to Bromhead's warning that 'some dead will be seen' by answering 'C'est la guerre, on ne peut pas avoir la guerre sans les morts'.

Bromhead's Diary vividly conveys the hazardous conditions in which he travelled with Greengrass and Gregoriev's replacement, Varlet, on this extended tour by rail, motor car and ship. The frightful 'fight and scramble' while waiting two hours on the platform at Tiflis for his train to Erzerum made him recall Delhi Station during the Durbar (which he had filmed), while the night voyage from Trebizond to Batum took him through the U-boat-patrolled waters of the Black Sea. Between screenings he continued to cut and rejoin his films, presumably in response to audience reactions although his jottings never say. One particular screening was held high in the Caucasus: 'Show at 6 o'clock is A.1. Rather cold but lovely night. Unique setting, mountains all round – troops high on hill and a few Kurdish tribesmen on hills wondering what it all means.' (28/11/16)

Bromhead arrived the next evening in a 'queer Turkish village' near Erzingan where the Colonel had not been forewarned of the Englishman's visit so that the screen had to be rigged up on a tree 'after much delay and axe cutting of branches'.

Bromhead repeatedly demonstrated his ability to improvise in such situations and clearly enjoyed making new acquaintances, a prerequisite in the remote areas he was now visiting. He could also extricate himself from difficulty, as happened for example on one occasion

Field HQ Staff of Russian Caucasian Army at Erzerum, November 1916. Captain Bromhead seated between Colonel Noskov in centre and Captain Bonegakof on left. Q114367

in Trebizond where he was 'waylaid' by a Russian captain and war correspondent who insisted on screening his own films after Bromhead's, thus spoiling the show by making it too long. (10/12/16) The following evening the motor mysteriously stopped just as the first Russian film went on, enabling the show to end with the customary speech by the Colonel and cheers for the respective armies and sovereigns. (11/12/16)

The February Revolution

After a break of four months in England Bromhead returned to Russia in April 1917 to a political and military situation transformed by the February Revolution and the abdication of the Tsar. The change was already apparent on the journey, for by coincidence the British propagandist travelled back to the Finland Station in Petrograd in the same train that was taking another future film propagandist, Lenin, back to his own country. Bromhead confided his personal distaste for his fellow travellers to his Diary:

> They are all over the place- very noisy and assertive – also the ugliest lot of people I ever saw. (14/4/17)

He also noticed that the earlier spirit of doubt towards Britain and France had been replaced by a deepening antagonism:

> Socialist Lenin and 30 Russians from Switzerland on train. Manifestation at every station, mostly worked up by the party in

question. Lenin and others addressed soldiers and crowd several times, mostly very anti-war and anti-British/French. His speeches almost always contained references to British and French Capitaliski Bourgeoisie. I had no trouble anywhere with Customs and got whisky through safely. (16/4/17)

The effect of the February Revolution on British propaganda policy towards Russia was profound. *The Report on the Work of the Anglo-Russian Commission, February to June 1917* noted that propaganda now needed to be carried out on a joint Allied basis rather than separately (as had previously been the case) in order to meet the much more active hostility of the Russians. Expenditure should be raised so that the increasing amount of German propaganda could be countered. The original causes of the War had been forgotten, and it was Britain which was now accused of being imperialistic and perceived as hostile to the current debate about peace aims. [34]

British official war films were not well suited to these new requirements of propaganda, although mention in Bromhead's Diary (12/5/17) that M. Jeannot, President of French Propaganda, had indicated himself 'willing to show English films round the schools with French films' does suggest that in one area at least, that of cooperation between the two powers, a new spirit had taken the place of previous rivalry. Bromhead promptly agreed to send him one of the old copies of *Britain Prepared*.

Allied war films directed at a population tired of war and hostile to outside efforts of encouragement now risked not merely being ineffective but actually counterproductive. While Bromhead continued to promote such recent British films as *The Battle of the Ancre and the Advance of the Tanks* (released in London on 15 January 1917), and to arrange for their commercial handling through different concessionaires according to territory, the variety of Russian reactions to such battle films can be gauged from an ironic piece titled 'Manslaughter' from the newspaper *Pravda* of 17th June, forwarded to Wellington House in the quaint translation which follows:

Sir Buchanan, the English Ambassador, kindly asked us to enjoy the films on the cinematograph showing the pictures of the famous British Tanks, the land dreadnoughts.

For this kindness we are grateful. We went

and we saw. In England machines are magnificently made. Machines mounted with guns varying from 6 inches to 18 inches calibre, capable of spitting forth tens of pounds of deadly metals – they work as sowing machines sow. Their masters stand near them, working mechanics dressed in khaki blouses, working in order to stagger the world, playing their parts well. But this is only the first act.

In the second act we see the victims OF THE WORK of these magnificent machines and skilled mechanics – ONLY GERMANS. Endless lines of strechers [sic] on which are carried mutilated bodies, the mutilated and distorted faces of the dead, caused such an impression, that even the 'triumphant' public forgot to applaud. The same despondent impression prevailed during the showing of the German trenches filled with corpses. The 'triumphant' spirit was broken.

This spirit was manifested very warmly on the representation of the explosion of a mine, on which the miner, an Australian workman, had worked FOR ONE YEAR, and another on which six months was spent.

At this appallingly destructive waste of labour, worthy ladies and gentlemen evinced the most extravagant flights of ecstasy.

This frenzied ecstasy increased tenfold at the sight of these 'manslaughters', land dreadnoughts, bearing resemblance to some antediluvian monster. These gigantic machines armed with guns, crushing everything in their path, undergrowth, trenches, wire-entanglements.

The skill of the English workman is beyond all doubt. But it is a shame that the fruits of their skill are shown only to young ladies and worthy people. They should be shown to the workmen and peasants of all the belligerent countries because the first idea which would come into their heads would be: 'Is it possible that the workmen are so stupid as to waste their skill, brains and labour on the construction of such exterminators of mankind, they could create an arm of advantageous labour, which would introduce new elements of life. DOWN WITH THIS HUMILIATING WASTE AND PERVERTION [SIC] OF HUMAN LABOUR. DOWN WITH THIS DISGUSTING, OBJECTLESS AND CRIMINAL FRATRICIDE. DOWN <u>WITH THE WAR</u>.

It is a great shame that splendid English workmen and foremen should thus throw away their strength and knowledge. But the English Colonel to some extent reassures us; 'In expectation of an offensive on your part, we like you – but if you refuse to attack, then ...'

However, he added, that 'unfortunately' on their front there were only volunteers – 5 million volunteers – and that universal military service raised 'very few troops'. And as we know that in England there are massed lock-outs one after the other, therefore it is evident that the reserve of 'defenders' must be already exhausted.

We will now hope that our English comrades will forge 'tanks' not for fratricidal war, but for the destruction of the 'barbed wire entanglements' of the capitalists. [35]

The Head of the Foreign Office News Department, C H Montgomery, reacted to this review by confidently asserting 'There is always a risk of film exhibitions being misused in this way but it is more than counterbalanced by the good they do.' (20/7/17) His superior in the Foreign Office agreed, and Bromhead's work continued. [36]

Fifth screening tour: Rumania

Having spent three months in Petrograd and Moscow arranging such film shows as that described by Pravda's journalist and forwarding a proposal to London for specially equipped cine-motors to visit the provinces, Bromhead left by train for his fifth and final tour, to Rumania (20th July – 23rd August), as street fighting broke out in the capital. He was accompanied by Greengrass and his new projectionist Prout, whom he photographed erecting the screen for open air shows, and was assisted in Rumania by two Propaganda Majors of the British Military Mission to Rumania, Fitzwilliams and Keyes.

The reaction to the screenings was no longer as uniformly favourable as in the past. Although Bromhead was told by a Russian lieutenant that his fellow officers considered the 'shows most useful and helpful to them in their work' (6/8/17) he could not but note the poor morale in both the Russian and Rumanian Armies, who had to attend separate shows:

> Passed about 1200 Russian transport carts en route and Rumanians on way up to take over. Picture of Russians retreating singing and Rumanians plodding quietly to front. (4/8/17)

After an open air show at Roman to reserve battalions of the Russian 9th Army, he observed:

> Arrangements made by Major Keyes and Fitzwilliams very satisfactory, light good and about 8/10,000 people present but not very enthusiastic. This is a bad army – discipline and conditions rotten. (1/8/17)

On his return to Petrograd on 23 August Bromhead viewed the latest films from London:

> Went Kapelli and saw new films – they are very poor. *Péronne* and *Bapaume* – both alike, all ruins. Negative only of *Battle of Arras*, saw part of it but no description or details. (25/8/17)

Even if Bromhead had had more suitable films to show, the political instability and military uncertainty in Russia made further screening tours impracticable, and a proposed trip to Helsingfors was indefinitely postponed. He therefore tidied up in Petrograd and returned to London. [37] Although he tried to revive his mission after the Bolshevik Revolution together with the mobile cinema teams he had earlier proposed, he was recalled while en route to Russia via Sweden in January 1918. [38] As the Pravda journalist had predicted, if the persuasive power of Bromhead's films were to fail in Russia, the British could still try to influence events through direct military intervention.

Bromhead's achievement

Bromhead's own personal achievement was clearly considerable. As a pioneer film propagandist, his long experience of the commercial cinema in Britain enabled him to test in one very diverse society Wellington House's theory that film could be effectively exported to

Captain Bromhead's orderly Private Greengrass, Major Keyes' Cossack orderly Pashenko and Private Prout, Bromhead's projectionist on his Rumanian tour, August 1917. Q114356

Screen erected outside British Hospital at Roman, Rumania for film show by Captain Bromhead to wounded, public and soldiers at 10pm on 6 August 1917. 'Good show after dinner at hospital. I yelled description in French which was translated into Rumanian.' Major Keyes and Major Fitzwilliams stand in rear. Q114361

Captain Bromhead's cinema lorry with Major Keyes, Cossack driver and Private Greengrass near Piatra Neamt, Rumania, August 1917. Q114357

Private Greengrass and Private Prout fix screen before its erection at Poltinossa, 13 August 1917. 'Russian sappers, a very useful lot at this place, are helping.' Q114360

Cinema lorry facing screen at Bekazal, Rumania, August 1917. Q114358

Soldiers of 15th Regiment, 4th Division fixing screen at Poltinossa pitch, Bukovina, Austro-Hungary, 13 August 1917. Q114359

allied and neutral countries. Although it is clear that the French were also touring their own official films in Russia, and it is known that the Salvation Army considered an open air show to an audience of 20,000 practicable [39], Bromhead was experimenting entirely unassisted. As he wrote in August 1916:

> This work is very arduous, especially singlehanded, and at such a long way from one's base… I can consult no one who can advise me and simply go on doing the best I can in my own judgement. [40]

Bromhead's screenings to the Tsar and his generals provided this new medium, which had originated as fair-ground entertainment, with a respectability and credibility essential to its subsequent development as a powerful means of persuasion. The eventual abandonment of his mission to Russia should not be taken to indicate that his film propaganda had failed – even the hostile Pravda witness acknowledged that the British film was well received by one section of society – but rather as self-evident proof that the power of any

form of propaganda can be limited by the course of events.

At this early stage in the history of cinema Bromhead's knowledge of all aspects of film performance was probably a more important factor in his success than the nature of what he was showing his largely captive audiences. He may have been frustrated that his requests for more timely and suitable material were not granted, but the subsequent history of war film has generally revealed that there is an inevitable gulf between what the cameraman records and what the propagandist thinks is necessary for his own purpose. He may also have been unfortunate that the evolution in British official films from reels showing fixed images of self-confident military, naval and industrial power to the more destructive scenes of the subsequent battle films should have been moving counter to the changing mood in Russia, but it would be anachronistic to expect films to have been specially tailored and targetted to specific countries at this early date. [41]

Bromhead's Reports were so well received by Wellington House that his mission was held up as a model for similar work by its other Agents for

Lt Colonel Bromhead receives message for Italian Armies from King George V outside Buckingham Palace on 4 May 1918 prior to Mission to Italy. Q114369

Cinematograph Propaganda, notably in France and Italy. The Reports did of course confirm its own long-held conviction that film was a vital propaganda medium and also highlighted the official, though not commercial, success of their Cinema Committee's own first, and what turned out to be their only, film production.

Bromhead's own career [42] provides a thread of continuity in film propaganda history, for in the Second World War he was appointed Honorary Adviser to the Ministry of Information Films Division together with Sidney Bernstein of Granada Cinemas. [43] Both men were able to provide the essential link between the official propagandists in Senate House and the commercial network of distribution and exhibition through which films are channelled to their audiences. British official films and newsreels were again sent to Russia (in exchange for Soviet documentaries and newsreels) but no longer with the certainty that they would be viewed by an audience even a fraction the size of Bromhead's in the First World War.

Notes

1. *Second Report on the Work Conducted for the Government at Wellington House*, February 1916, p 5.
2. *Colonel A C Bromhead Russian Diaries 1916 and 1917*, edited by J Bromhead, September 1972. Copies deposited in the IWM Department of Documents and Senate House, University of London Library, which also has the manuscript diaries.
3. *Second Report*, op cit, p 6.
4. Hans Barkhausen, *Filmpropaganda für Deutschland im Ersten und Zweiten Weltkrieg*, Georg Olms Verlag, Hildesheim, 1982, p 24. The German Consul in Amsterdam complained in October 1915 that impressive French film of the war was being screened but that there were no German films to satisfy the Dutch public's reported interest in Russian prisoners.
5. Nicholas Reeves, *Official British Film Propaganda During The First World War*, Croom Helm, Beckenham, 1986, pp 89-94.
6. *Second Report*, op cit, p 7.
7. *Second Report.* op cit, p 5.
8. Rachael Low and Roger Manvell, *The History of the British Film 1896-1906*, Unwin, London, 1948, p 21.
9. Ibid, p 38.
10. *Who's Who, 1945*, p 334. Entry for Lieut-Colonel Alfred Claude Bromhead, CBE 1918. (1876-1963). Acquired British control and became chairman of Gaumont Company, 1922, then first Chairman of Gaumont British Picture Corporation.
11. Buchanan to Montgomery, 14 January 1916, PRO, FO 371/2824.
12. Ibid, Gowers to Montgomery, 14 January 1916.
13. Ibid, Buchanan to Montgomery, 8 January 1916.
14. Ibid, Montgomery to Buchanan, 6 January 1916.
15. Ibid, Bromhead to Cinema Committee, 11 February 1916.
16. Jay Leyda, *Kino; A History of the Russian and Soviet Film*, Allen and Unwin, London, 1960, p 87.
17. Quoted in the above, pp 86-87.
18. Bromhead to Welsh, 10 February 1916, PRO, FO 371/2824.
19. *Who's Who*, 1969, p 1672. Bruce married in 1917 Tamara Karsavina, Prima Ballerina at the Mariinsky Theatre, 1902-19.
20. Jay Leyda, op cit, p 30 and p 90.
21. *Letters of the Tsaritsa to the Tsar 1914-1916*, Duckworth, London, 1923, p 310.
22. J C Trewin, *Tutor to the Tsarevich: An Intimate Portrait of the Last Days of the Russian Imperial Family, compiled from the papers of Charles Sydney Gibbes*, Macmillan, London, 1975, pp 42-43 and p 46.
23. Jay Leyda, op cit, p 90.
24. Department of Documents, papers of Admiral Sir Richard Phillimore, 66/9/1/.
25. Bromhead to Cinema Committee, 11 February 1916, PRO FO 371/2824.
26. *Third Report on the Work Conducted for the Government at Wellington House*, September 1916, p 102.
27. Bromhead to Cinema Committee, Report No. 8, 4 July 1916, PRO FO 395/25.
28. Bromhead to Cinema Committee, Report No. 9, 11 July 1916, PRO FO 395/25.
29. Bromhead to Cinema Committee, Report No. 10, 16 August 1916, PRO FO 395/25.
30. Gowers to Montgomery, 15 June 1916, PRO FO 395/25.
31. Gowers to Montgomery, 29 September 1916, PRO FO 395/25.
32. Bromhead to Gowers, 19 September 1916, PRO FO 395/25.
33. Bromhead to Cinema Committee, Report No. 11, 25 September 1916, PRO FO 395/25.
34. PRO FO 395/106.
35. Ibid.
36. Ibid.
37. Sixteen of Bromhead's film prints and negatives were returned to London from the British Embassy in Leningrad in 1926, and passed to the Imperial War Museum. The list notes which films had Russian titles or required new titles and includes mention of one unknown film 'stuck together and useless'. Since originals of these films were already held by the Museum, and since only the images and not the titles were then considered of historic value, this detailed evidence of Bromhead's activity was lost to the historian. How films ever survive to be archivally preserved and researched would be another article. See Correspondence in Department of Film, Foster to Foxen-Cooper, 23 August 1926.
38. Adrian Brunel, *Nice Work: The Story of Thirty Years in British Film Production*, Forbes Robertson, London, 1949, p 43.
39. *War Lecturer's Handbook*, Simla, 2nd Edn, 1918?, p 12. In an Appendix, Commissioner Booth-Tucker of the Salvation Army comments on the practical aspects of organising travelling Moving Picture shows in India, and recommends the use of portable equipment from America, where 'special motor cars are equipped to travel all over the country and give exhibitions of moving pictures of a useful educational character'.
40. Bromhead to Wilkinson, 19 August 1916, PRO FO 395/25.
41. Twenty years later Bromhead reportedly told entertaining stories about the unexpected reactions to the films from audiences in Russia too ignorant to grasp their significance, as, for example, when he showed films of the Royal Navy to Russians who had never seen the sea nor knew Britain's naval record. See Sidney Rogerson, *Propaganda in the Next War*, Geoffrey Bles, London, 1938, p 110.
42. Bromhead headed the British Military Cinematograph Mission to Italy from May to December 1918. The Mission later screened British Battle films to former Italian prisoners of war to counter their previous exposure to Austrian propaganda, 'to break down any Bolshevik tendencies which may have been formed during the period of incarceration' and to show the contribution of Britain, rather than of the 'ubiquitous American', to the Allied victory. See Circular Letter to all Officers, British Military Cinematograph Mission, 8 January 1919, in *Colonel A C Bromhead Russian Diaries 1916 and 1917.*
43. Caroline Moorehead, *Sidney Bernstein: A Biography*, Jonathan Cape, London, 1984.

Further reading

Kevin Brownlow, *The War, The West and The Wilderness*, Secker and Warburg, London, 1978.
Robert Bruce Lockhart, *Memoirs of a British Agent*, Harmondsworth, London, 1950.
Rupert Hart-Davis ed., *The Autobiography of Arthur Ransome*, Jonathan Cape, London, 1976.
Bernard Pares, *Russian Memoirs*, Jonathan Cape, London, 1931.
M L Sanders and Philip M Taylor, *British Propaganda during the First World War*, Macmillan, London, 1982.
M L Sanders, British Film Propaganda in Russia, 1916-1918, *Historical Journal of Film, Radio and Television, Vol 3, No. 2*, 1983.
Roger Smither ed., *Imperial War Museum Film Catalogue. Volume I: The First World War Archive*, Flicks Books, Trowbridge, 1994.

Acknowledgement

The author is grateful to Dr John Screen, Librarian, School of Slavonic and East European Studies, University of London, for the loan for copying by the Department of Photographs of Bromhead's original prints and negatives, which illustrate this article, and for an English translation of his article on British Film Propaganda to Russian Troops in Finland in 1916 from *Sotilasaikakauslehti* (Helsinki), Vol. 58, No. 4, 1983: Kuinka 'Englanti on valmis' tuli Suomeen vuonna 1916'.

'A bit of campaign oratory': Wendell Willkie's visit to Britain, January 1941, and the fight for Lend-Lease

Terry Charman

Terry Charman is a research assistant in the Research and Information Office.

I am here as Wendell Willkie, I am representing no one. I am very glad to be in England for whose cause I have the utmost sympathy. I want to do all I can to get the United States to give England the utmost aid possible in her struggle for free men all over the world. [1]

In these days of shuttle diplomacy it is hard to realize the impact made on both sides of the Atlantic by Wendell Willkie, America's 'Private Citizen Number One', during his trip to embattled Britain in January 1941. Barely known outside business circles a year previously, he had captured the Republican Party nomination for presidential candidate at the convention in Philadelphia in June 1940. In the subsequent contest against Franklin Roosevelt, standing for a record breaking third term, Willkie had proved a formidable campaigner, attacking the New Deal and the tardiness of America's defence preparations under the Democratic Party's régime.

Willkie had made no attempt to disguise his feelings about Nazism:

> I clearly asserted my position against race hatred, bigotry and Hitlerism... long before I even thought of being a presidential candidate. I did it solely because I wanted to express my protest against all Fascistic persecution methods. If anti-semitism should spread its roots in the United States as it had done... in Europe then it would definitely be a calamity for the United States. [2]

The German Chargé d' Affaires in Washington, Dr Hans Thomsen, reported back to Berlin:

> From the standpoint of foreign policy, Willkie's nomination is unfortunate for us. He is not an isolationist, and his attitude in the past permits no doubt that he belongs to those Republicans who see America's best defence in supporting England by all means short of war. [3]

In the event Roosevelt won his third term by 27,241,939 votes to Willkie's 22,327,226, but the defeated candidate

October 24, 1942

PICTURE
POST

HULTON'S NATIONAL WEEKLY
In this issue: WENDELL WILLKIE 4D

OCTOBER 24, 1942   by REBECCA WEST   Vol. 17. No. 4

Willkie's natural exuberance was well displayed on the front cover of *Picture Post*'s 24th
October 1942 issue. Rebecca West had hosted a dinner for Willkie during his 1941 visit
to Britain.

had polled more votes than any previous one with the exception of FDR himself, who told his son James, 'I'm happy I've won, but I'm sorry Wendell lost'. [4] Willkie immediately telegraphed Roosevelt:

Congratulations on your re-election as President of the United States. I know that we both are gratified that so many American citizens participated in the election. I wish you all personal health and happiness. Cordially Wendell L Willkie [5]

Later he said in a broadcast:

I accept the result of the election with complete goodwill. I extend my thanks... to the millions who supported me. I know that they will continue, as I shall, to work for the unity of our people in the completion of our defence programme, and in the sending of aid to Great Britain. [6]

Such a good sportsmanlike attitude went down well in Britain, where Willkie's nomination had been recognised as 'one of the minor miracles of which the Allied cause stands in need', [7] but where nevertheless Roosevelt's victory was greeted with relief. Diarist and socialite 'Chips' Channon wrote in his diary: 'President Roosevelt has had an even greater triumph than anyone anticipated. A real landslide, and I have yet to see anyone who is not delighted.' [8]

For the next few weeks Willkie rested after the exertions of the campaign, but with Roosevelt's introduction of the Lend-Lease Bill he was determined that military aid to Britain would become his next political cause. He took this stance despite the fact that almost all the rest of the Republican Party leadership was aligned in opposition to Lend-Lease. Roosevelt compared his scheme to lending a garden hose to a neighbour whose house was on fire, but Senator Robert Taft countered, 'Lending war equipment is a good deal like lending chewing gum. You don't want it back.' Senator Charles McNary, who had been Willkie's running mate as Vice-Presidential candidate, was opposed to Lend-Lease, believing it gave 'extraordinary and total power to one man' and Thomas Dewey, Willkie's great rival and the Republican candidate against FDR in 1944 felt that Lend-Lease 'would bring an end to free government in the US.' [9] Willkie summed up his attitude in a letter:

I remained silent after the campaign for a

Willkie arrives at 'a western port' on 26 January 1941. 'I am very glad to be here in England' he told reporters,'for whose cause I have the utmost sympathy.' HU65262

couple of months, making only off the record talks about my views, but when Messrs. Hoover, Landon, Dewey Taft and Vandenberg all came out in a frontal assault on the Lend-Lease Bill, I thought I owed a duty to speak for it. [10]

On 13 January 1941 he made a public statement of his views:

'It is the history of democracy that under dire circumstances, extraordinary powers must be granted to the elected Executive. Democracy cannot hope to defend itself in any other way... The United States is not a belligerent, and we hope shall not be. Our problem, however, is not alone to keep America out of war, but to keep war out of America... Appeasers, isolationists, or lip service friends of Britain will seek to sabotage the programme of aid to Britain and her allies behind the screen of opposition to this bill. [11]

At the same time Willkie announced his intention to visit Britain, explaining:

> I was writing an article, and I put down a statement about Great Britain. Then I thought, how do I know that? The idea popped into my head, why not go to the source? Why not go to England and find out?

In fact the idea that Willkie should undertake such a trip had been going the rounds of official Washington for some time. William Stephenson, the Canadian born British intelligence chief is said to have made the initial suggestion to Roosevelt who liked the idea as he 'felt that the leader of the opposition would carry more reassurance than a political friend of the President's,' according to Secretary of Labor, Frances Perkins. [12] At a New Year's party Judge Felix Frankfurter broached the idea to Willkie's close friend Irita Van Doren, who in turn passed it on to Willkie. As it coincided with his own methods of meeting people and assessing situations for himself, he readily adopted the idea, and telephoned Secretary of State Cordell Hull in order to obtain a passport. An hour and forty minute conference with Hull ensued to be followed by a meeting with Roosevelt himself on 19 January 1941, the night before FDR's third inauguration. The two men got on well together and 'great bursts of laughter could be heard coming through the closed doors'. [13] Willkie left with a handwritten letter for Churchill from the President:

> Wendell Willkie will give you this, he is truly helping to keep politics out over here. I think this verse (of Longfellow's) applies to you as it does to us
>
> Sail on, O Ship of State
> Sail on, O Union strong and great!
> Humanity with all its fears
> With all its hopes of future years
> Is hanging breathless on thy fate. [14]

Three days later, at 8.30am on 22 January 1941 at La Guardia Airport, Willkie boarded the Pan American 'Yankee Clipper' for the first stage of his flight to Britain, a 'journey that captured the imagination of people on both sides of the Atlantic' according to political writer Marquis W Childs of *St Louis Post Dispatch*. Willkie arrived in London on 26 January and from the start was given the red carpet treatment by both the British establishment and people. The wife of the Greek Minister wrote in her diary: 'What sort of reception would Wendell Willkie have had if he had come on an official visit, considering what was happening to him as a private individual?' [15] His first full day was typical, after telling newspaper reporters when asked if he was pessimistic about the war 'I am never pessimistic', he set off from the Dorchester Hotel to an 11.15am meeting with Foreign Secretary Anthony Eden. Eden recalled that he had suggested that in order to find out what the British people really thought, he should speak to them whenever he got the chance. Their meeting finished, Eden escorted Willkie to the lift:

> As we stepped out a workman was patching some broken windows after an air raid. 'There,' I said, 'You can make a start now.' Willkie walked up to him and asked a few questions. The man had no idea who Willkie was.
>
> 'How do you feel about this war?'
>
> 'How d'yer mean?'
>
> Willkie persisted: 'Want to go through with it?'
>
> The man looked at him quickly: 'Hitler ain't dead yet, is he?' and turned back to his work. I could not have staged it as well. [16]

At midday Willkie left to view bomb damage in the City, and at 1.30pm lunched with Churchill. 'Don't ask me what we ate - fish, I think; I was too interested talking to notice,' Willkie told reporters. [17] At 3.45pm he was meeting Minister of Labour Ernest Bevin, before a break back at the hotel was followed by a 7.00pm press conference at the Ministry of Information and dinner with Lord and Lady Stamp. His visit to the devastated City had made a profound effect:

> I think it's very significant that the publishing area around Paternoster Row has been so badly blitzed. That's where the truth is told and the Nazis don't like the truth. [18]

He praised the civil defence workers as 'the finest men I've ever met' and stated 'I like their spirit. I think they're great, but then I didn't expect anything else.' [19]

The next day was taken up with meeting Labour Party Leaders Clement Attlee and Arthur Greenwood, the Governor of the Bank of England, Montagu Norman and Chancellor of the Exchequer Sir

'I am certain now that this country is united in an unbelievable way. No other nation in the world could have been so united in a cause as you are.' So said Willkie in a speech at Manchester on 3 February 1941. Cartoon reproduced by kind permission of the *Daily Mail* Solo Syndication.

" I LIKE THEIR NERVE "

Kingsley Wood. A visit to the House of Commons during the debate on the banning of the Communist newspaper the *Daily Worker* impressed Willkie greatly:

> It's really democracy working when a debate on the Freedom of the press is going on in the middle of an air raid. [20]

He was also impressed by the spirit of the ordinary Londoners whom he met while touring the air raid shelters. He told reporters:

> I'm a pretty hard boiled egg, I think, but this moves me deeply. I am almost spilling over.

and when a Londoner called out, 'We can take it, you go home and tell them that', Willkie replied, 'I most certainly will'. [21] The next day was one of contrasts. In the morning Willkie visited a typical London pub, the Chesterfield Arms, pulled the pumps, drank the beer, ('and darned good beer it was too'), with five soldiers before playing darts with Acton bricklayer Albert Phillips ('that guy was just too good for me'). That night he dined with Minister of Information Duff Cooper and his wife the legendary Lady Diana who wrote:

> London was excited and electrified by the Wendell Willkie visit. He went down into the Underground at night and down like a dinner with the crowds. They shout and cheer and say 'Tell them we can take it!' and 'Send us everything you can!' And this elephantine figure, with a painted white tin helmet, seems to amuse and impress them. I gave a dinner party for him (only ten of us) in a private room at the Dorchester... Willkie was treated like a king and film star rolled into one. The newspapers told us what he ate for breakfast and what size boots he wore. Now he has gone, I waved him goodbye last night and I pray God he will give a good account of us and our country, our needs and hopes, when he comes to testify to the Senate. [22]

On 2 February Willkie visited Coventry, devastated after the German air raid of 14 November 1940. On viewing the ruins of the cathedral he commented:

'I came here to listen, not to make speeches,' Willkie told the Ministry of Information's press conference on 27 January 1941. Sir Walter Monckton, the Ministry's Director General sits besides Willkie. HU65263'

It certainly is terrible, it is an outrage. But there seems no depression no matter whom you talk to. [23]

On the third he went to Liverpool and Manchester where he received a reception 'usually reserved for film stars and royalty' with crowds of 10,000 people greeting him with shouts: 'We carry on, you send the stuff'. Always with the common touch, he was photographed with a Private Price of the Pioneer Corps. 'Now,' Willkie joked, 'all the beautiful girls all over the world will write to you.' [24] The next day at 7.30am he flew to Dublin for a meeting with Irish Prime Minister Eamon De Valera, before returning to take tea (actually Scotch and soda) with King George VI and Queen Elizabeth. 'You are doing a better job on me than you did on another person,' he joked with the Queen, in an oblique reference to former Ambassador Joseph P Kennedy, notorious for his isolationist views. The Queen replied, 'Well, Mr Willkie, it wasn't because I didn't try on him.' [25]

In his biographer's words, 'As the Queen responded to him, simply and naturally, so did almost everybody in England. He took the country by storm. His visit became nothing less than a love affair between him and the English people.' [26] Of them he said, 'I have never in my life seen so united a people.' [27]

The evening following his Royal visit, writer Rebecca West gave a dinner in Willkie's honour where the guests included a number of leading intellectuals including J B Priestley, Julian Huxley and *New Statesman* editor Kingsley Martin. Also present was Harold Nicolson, diarist and Parliamentary Secretary to the Ministry of Information, who recorded his impressions of the evening:

> I sit next to Willkie. He is not tired but he is evidently bored. He turns his charm on but drums with his fingers… he says that his two major impressions are (1) Cohesion in the country. He is amazed that Big Business are as determined on victory as anybody… (2) Leadership. He quite saw that in normal times Winston might be a 'lousy' Prime Minister, but today not only was he superb in himself, but the Labour people all recognized his superiority. I could see what had struck him most was the patriotism of the capitalists…. a very attractive man. [28]

Willkie told the assembled company how he had urged De Valera that morning to allow the Royal Navy use of Irish ports. When the Irish premier had admitted that he wanted Britain to win, but was afraid that Dublin would be bombed if the ports were handed over, Willkie did not conceal his contempt. [29] While in London Willkie had met Harry Hopkins, Roosevelt's right-hand man, who was in Britain in order to assess her Lend-Lease requirements. Willkie told Hopkins that he would be prepared to undertake a testimony in favour of the Lend-Lease Bill before the Senate Committee on Foreign Relations. With the outcome of the Lend-Lease vote far from certain, Roosevelt took Willkie up on his offer, and Cordell Hull cabled him in Dublin to cut short his trip and return to Washington. Accordingly, Willkie left Britain on 5 February full of praise for Britain, its people and prime minister: 'Britain has been almost miraculously fortunate in her leadership at one of the supreme critical moments of history'. The feeling was mutual:

> Everywhere and with everyone he has left the impression of sincerity, friendship, boundless energy and radiant high spirits which has been most heartening. [30]

Churchill thought him a 'most able and forceful man' and Eden, who had entertained initial doubts, wrote: ' I am sure he is sincere in his desire to help and belief in our cause, while the courage of our people has moved him deeply. It has been a great gain to us that he should have come.' [31] Before leaving Willkie recorded a message for the German people to be broadcast by the BBC. In it he told how his ancestors had fled Germany to escape political repression and although he was

...proud of my German blood ...I hate aggression and tyranny... Tell the German people that we German-Americans reject and hate the aggression and lust for power of the present German government. [32]

On 9 February Willkie arrived back at La Guardia Airport telling the large crowd of reporters and wellwishers that it had been 'the most stimulating experience in my life'. Two days later Willkie appeared in the Caucus Room of the Senate Office building, jammed with nearly twelve hundred people, to give his testimony on the Lend-Lease Bill. He had been preceded by many in favour of the Bill such as Cordell Hull and Henry Stimson and also by its opponents, the most famous of whom was Colonel Charles Lindbergh, Atlantic flier, and now a leading luminary in the isolationist America First organisation.

Although showing obvious signs of travel strain, Willkie adopted his usual confident stance before the Committee. He announced that in his view Lend-Lease offered the United States 'the best clear chance' to avoid war. 'If Britain,' he declared, 'can stand through the summer then at last the effects of our long term assistance will begin to be felt. Reinforced by our gigantic resources Britain may be able to achieve that effectiveness which the democratic peoples have temporarily lost'. [33] He concluded with a vision of an 'open world... a world in which Americans will share with other nations the responsibilities - and the great prospect - of peace'. To achieve that state, Willkie argued 'We must bravely do the things that we know ought to be done.' [34]

Willkie faced a barrage of hostile questions from the isolationist senators on the Committee including those from his own party like Arthur Vandenberg who had sarcastically dubbed him 'The Clipper Ambassador'. But it was Senator Bennett Champ Clark of Missouri who was the most relentless in his cross-examination, although a lighter moment was reached when Clark called Willkie 'Mr President'. Laughing, Willkie quickly responded, 'Senator, you merely speak of what should have been'. Clark's methods were to bring up Willkie's campaign charges that Roosevelt would lead America into war if re-elected. Willkie responded that he saw no constructive purpose in discussing his old campaign speeches:

> I struggled hard as I could to beat Franklin Roosevelt and I tried to keep from pulling any of my punches. He was elected President. He is my President now. I expect to disagree with him whenever I please. [35]

This response which drew much applause from the spectators. In his questioning Senator Nye of North Dakota returned to the same theme as Clark, asking Willkie if he stood by his speech of 30 October 1940 in which he had predicted that FDR would have America at war by April 1941. 'It might be' Willkie replied. 'It was a bit of campaign oratory. I am very glad you read my speeches, because the President said he did not.' [36] The refreshing candour of this response met with laughter and applause, and interventionist William Allen White praised Willkie saying:

> I think one of the most courageous things any man ever said in public life was Willkie's campaign oratory statement. It was not discreet, but it was deeply honest. [37]

This view was not shared however by Republican Party chieftains, and for the rest of his short life it would be used against Willkie by his isolationist and conservative opponents. But whatever influence he had lost among the bosses of the Republican Party was more than offset by his increased prestige among those who had voted against him in 1940. Senator Hiram Johnson might denounce Willkie's appearance as 'a one-man circus intended to influence the citizens', but that was just what it did. According to the Gallup Poll, Willkie's testimony had helped to swing public opinion behind Lend-Lease, including a plurality of rank and file Republicans. Gallup also reported that 60% of American public opinion now

Willkie, about to take off for his return journey to the USA on 5 February 1941. His trip had convinced him 'that in the face of totalitarian attack, freemen feel a common brotherhood.' CH2063

On his 1942 inspection tour which resulted in the best selling book *One World*, Willkie met Montgomery, then a Lieutenant General, who was planning the Battle of El Alamein. 'It is now mathematically certain that I will eventually destroy Rommel,' Montgomery told Willkie. E16537

thought that he would have made a good president had he won in 1940. [38]

The day after Willkie testified, the Foreign Relations Committee recommended the passage of Lend-Lease by a vote of 15 to 8, and on March 8 1941 the Senate passed the Lend-Lease Bill by a vote of 60-31, with the Republicans voting 17-10 against it. One man was certain of Willkie's contribution to the success of the passage of the bill. To Harry Hopkins Franklin Roosevelt declared:

> We might not have had Lend-Lease ...if it hadn't been for Wendell Willkie. He was a godsend to the country when we needed him most. [39]

And in Berlin Dr Goebbels, Nazi propaganda minister, recorded in his diary:

> Willkie is revealing himself to an increasing extent as swine and a super-interventionist.

He has become a spokesman for Roosevelt's policies but rather more radical. [40]

Willkie never held office. Defeated in the Wisconsin presidential primary, he saw the 1944 Republican presidential candidacy go to Thomas E Dewey, a man he despised, before dying suddenly on 8 October 1944 at the age of only fifty-two.

Two years earlier, he had undertaken a trip around the battle fronts with even more far-reaching effects than his 1941 trip to Britain. As a result of his journey he had written *One World*, the war's biggest best-seller and a plea for both international co-operation and friendship together with American rejection of isolationism.

As one of his biographers put it, with Willkie's death 'people came to understand that a rare spirit had lived in their midst, a bright burning fire that had been extinguished, leaving the world a little colder and a little darker.' [41]

Notes

1. *News Chronicle*, 27 January 1941.
2. Herman O Makey, *Wendell Willkie of Elwood*, National Book Company, Elwood, Indiana, 1940, p 266.
3. Steve Neal, *Dark horse: a biography of Wendell Willkie*, Doubleday, Garden City, NY, 1984, p 120.
4. James Roosevelt, *My Parents*, Playboy Press, Chicago, 1976, p 164.
5. Gordon Beckles, *America chooses!*, Harrap, London, 1941, p 53.
6. Ibid, p 165.
7. Neal, op cit, p 120.
8. Robert Rhodes James (ed), *Chips: The Diaries of Sir Henry Channon*, Weidenfeld & Nicholson, London, 1967, p 273.
9. Neal, op cit, p 187.
10. Ibid, p 187.
11. Ellsworth Barnard, *Wendell Willkie: Fighter for Freedom*, North Michigan University Press, Marquette, Michigan, 1966, pp 275-276.
12. Neal, op cit, p 188.
13. James Roosevelt and Sidney Shallet, *Affectionately FDR*, Harcourt, Brace, New York, 1959, p 325.
14. Robert E Sherwood *The White House Papers of Harry L Hopkins: Volume 1 September 1939 - January 1942*, Eyre and Spottiswoode, London, 1948, p 235.
15. Charles Graves, *Off the Record*, Hutchinson, London, 1941, p 91.
16. The Earl of Avon, *The Eden Memoirs: The Reckoning*, Cassell, London, 1965, pp 253-254.
17. *News Chronicle*, 29 January 1941.
18. Ibid.
19. Ibid.
20. *News Chronicle*, 28 January 1941.
21. *News Chronicle*, 30 January 1941.
22. Diana Cooper, *Trumpets from the Steep*, Hart-Davis, London, 1960, p 72.
23. *News Chronicle*, 3 February 1941.
24. *News Chronicle*, 4 February 1941.
25. Barnard, op cit, p 281.
26. Ibid, p 281.
27. *News Chronicle*, 5 February 1941.
28. Harold Nicolson, *Diaries and Letters 1939-1945*, Collins Fontana, London, 1970, pp 139-140.
29. Ibid, p 140.
30. *The Times*, 6 February 1941.
31. Avon, op cit, p 254.
32. *War Illustrated*, Vol 4, 21 February 1941, p 188.
33. *"To Promote the defense of the United States": hearings before the Committee on Foreign Relations US Senate 11 February 1941*, Government Printing Office, Washington DC, 1941, pp 870-877.
34. Ibid, p 877.
35. Ibid, p 894.
36. Ibid, p 905.
37. Neal, op cit, p 206.
38. Ibid, p 206.
39. Sherwood, op cit, p 635.
40. Fred Taylor (ed), *The Goebbels Diaries 1939-1941*, Hamish Hamilton, London, 1982, p 234.
41. Irving Stone, *They Also Ran*, Doubleday, Garden City, NY, 1954, p 365.

Somme footnote : the Battle of the Ancre and the struggle for Frankfort Trench, November 1916

Peter Simkins

Field-Marshal Sir Douglas Haig (1861-1928), Commander-in-Chief of the British Expeditionary Force from December 1915 until the end of First World War. Q 23659

Peter Simkins is Head of the Museum's Research and Information Office.

On 18 November 1916, in the final phase of the Allied offensive on the Somme, the British 32nd Division attacked the Munich and Frankfort Trenches - which were situated on Redan Ridge, about one mile north-east of Beaumont Hamel - while other units attacked towards Grandcourt, south of the River Ancre. [1] Although the 19th Division reached the western edge of Grandcourt, the latter village was to remain in German hands until the following February. Similarly, as so often happened when the British launched attacks on a limited scale in 1916, the 32nd Division's assault on Munich and Frankfort Trenches was, in the main, a costly failure, despite the considerable gallantry and powers of endurance displayed by all ranks in dreadful conditions. By nightfall on 18 November, most of the survivors of the attack had fallen back to positions in or near their own front line. Remarkably, however, more than 100 other ranks and a handful of officers from the 11th Battalion, Border Regiment, and the 16th Battalion, Highland Light

Infantry, not only penetrated as far as Frankfort Trench but held out there, largely unaided, for eight days. This courageous stand in Frankfort Trench merits only a footnote in the British official history yet, like the 32nd Division's attack as a whole, the episode illustrates many of the best and worst features of the battlefield performance of the British Expeditionary Force (BEF) in 1916. [2]

Four and a half months earlier, the intention of General Sir Douglas Haig, the Commander-in-Chief of the BEF, had been that, in the opening stage of the Franco-British offensive, Lieutenant-General Sir Henry Rawlinson's Fourth Army should seize the German front line defences from Serre in the north to Montauban in the south. [3] It was then to strike at the German second position on the slopes in front of Miraumont and along the ridge line stretching between the Ancre, Pozières and Ginchy. If these attacks were successful, and the German third position in the Le Sars-Flers-Morval sector could subsequently be overrun, Bapaume would thereby be threatened and the way uncovered for the Reserve Army,

General Sir Hubert Gough (1870-1963) who, as a lieutenant-general, commanded the Reserve (or Fifth Army) on the Somme in 1916. Although widely regarded as a 'thruster', his conduct of operations on the Somme in 1916, and at Arras and Ypres in 1917, was undistinguished, and he was removed from command following the retreat of the Fifth Army in March 1918. Q 35825d

under Lieutenant-General Sir Hubert Gough, to exploit the situation and swing northward in the direction of Arras.

For the British, who, because of the pressure on the French at Verdun, were playing a leading role in an Allied offensive on the Western Front for the first time, the Battle of the Somme could scarcely have had a more disastrous beginning. Supported by a diversionary assault on Gommecourt by two divisions of the Third Army, Rawlinson's Fourth Army had attacked on an eighteen-mile front on 1 July 1916. On that first day, the only significant British gains were on the right, or southern flank, where the 18th and 30th Divisions, attacking alongside the French, captured all their objectives, including Montauban, and the 7th Division took Mametz. At Thiepval, the 36th (Ulster) Division initially managed to seize much of the Schwaben Redoubt - one of the most formidable German defensive bastions on the Western Front - but were obliged to withdraw by evening as the formations on its flanks had been unable to make corresponding progress. Indeed, immediately to its left, north of the Ancre, the units of VIII Corps had suffered heavily in a fruitless attempt to secure Beaumont Hamel, Redan Ridge and Serre, and had won only a temporary foothold in a German salient and strongpoint known as the Quadrilateral. The cost of the small advance on the Fourth Army's right on 1 July was a staggering 57,470 casualties, of whom 19,240 were killed - the highest losses ever sustained by the British Army in a single day. [4]

From 2 to 13 July, the Fourth Army sought to capitalise on its success on the right and to capture Contalmaison, Mametz Wood and Trones Wood in order to secure the flanks of an attack on part of the German second position. The assault in question was duly launched at dawn on 14 July after a daring night assembly in No Man's Land and a sudden intensification of the three-day preliminary bombardment in the last five minutes before zero hour. 6,000 yards of the German second position between Bazentin le Petit and Longueval quickly fell to the British but nearby Delville Wood and High Wood were held by the Germans until 27 August and 15 September respectively, robbing the Fourth Army's latest advance of much of its potential impact.

In the two months which followed the 14 July assault, the offensive developed into a grim battle of attrition. Haig himself came to accept that the prospects of an early breakthrough had receded, now seeing the BEF's operations on the Somme more in terms of a 'wearing-out' fight in preparation for the next large-scale set-piece assault, which was planned for mid-September

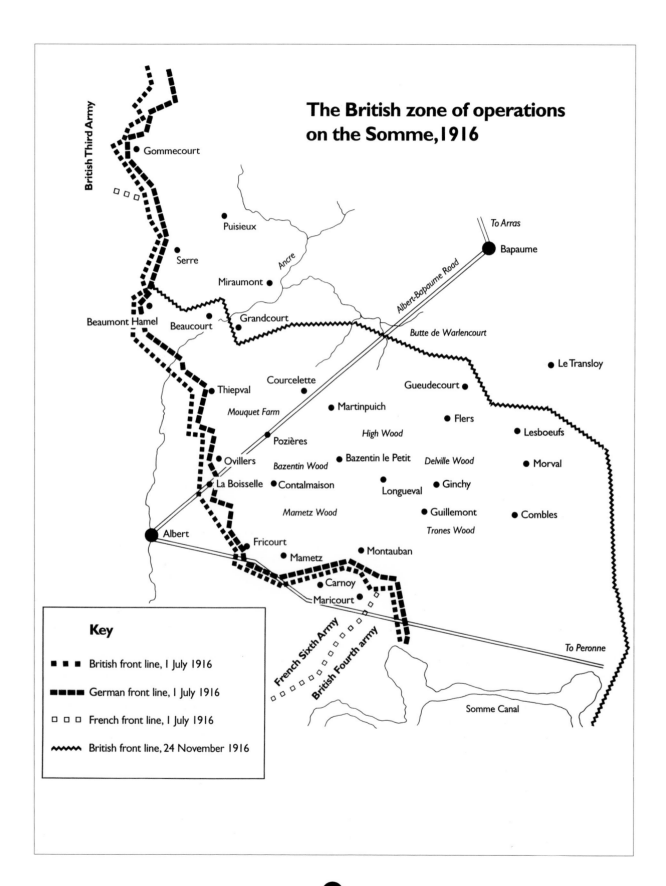

The British zone of operations on the Somme, 1916

British Third Army

Gommecourt

Puisieux

Serre

Ancre

Miraumont

To Arras

Bapaume

Albert-Bapaume Road

Butte de Warlencourt

Beaumont Hamel

Beaucourt

Grandcourt

Le Transloy

Courcelette

Gueudecourt

Thiepval

Mouquet Farm

Martinpuich

Flers

High Wood

Lesboeufs

Pozières

Bazentin le Petit

Delville Wood

Morval

Ovillers

Bazentin Wood

La Boisselle

Contalmaison

Longueval

Ginchy

Mametz Wood

Guillemont

Combles

Trones Wood

Albert

Fricourt

Mametz

Montauban

Carnoy

Maricourt

French Sixth Army

British Fourth army

To Peronne

Somme Canal

Key

■ ■ ■ British front line, 1 July 1916

▆▆▆▆ German front line, 1 July 1916

□ □ □ French front line, 1 July 1916

∿∿∿ British front line, 24 November 1916

and which Haig hoped would prove to be the decisive stroke. [5] During the period from 15 July to 14 September, the Fourth Army, apart from its repeated attempts to win Delville Wood and High Wood, was also embroiled in a bitter contest for Guillemont and Ginchy, both of which were captured in the first half of September. In the meantime, Gough's Reserve Army, which had gradually assumed responsibility for operations north of the Albert-Bapaume road, was beginning to figure more prominently in the offensive. After a fierce struggle, starting on 23 July, Australian troops of I Anzac Corps had, by 5 August, captured Pozières, on the Albert-Bapaume road, as well as the ruined mill on the ridge line beyond the village. The gains at Pozières undoubtedly provided the BEF with better observation over the central section of the battlefield, although the Australians suffered some 23,000 casualties in five weeks. Moreover, Pozières was only a prelude to the long and painful slogging match which the Reserve Army had still to face in order to take the successive German trench lines north-west of the Albert-Bapaume road, and on the slopes and spurs of the Morval-Grandcourt ridge, so that it could unlock the German defences at Thiepval from the rear.

A large proportion of the British attacks launched from mid July to early September were comparatively small-scale affairs, the aims of which were to push forward the British line at various points, to win local tactical advantages and to improve the starting positions for the major attack in mid-September. In a war dominated by artillery, it was often vital to straighten the start line before a big assault to ensure that the preliminary bombardment and supporting barrage would be as accurate as possible, but the price of such 'line straightening' operations was a serious erosion of the BEF's combat strength. In their outstanding recent analysis of Rawlinson's performance on the Somme, Robin Prior and Trevor Wilson have observed that, in sixty-two days, the Fourth Army lost around 82,000 men while advancing a mere 1,000 yards on a five-mile front. Only on some five occasions out of ninety operations were twenty or more battalions involved and only four attacks were delivered across the whole of the Fourth Army's front between 15 July and 14 September. [6] Gough too showed a predilection for frequent attacks with moderate numbers to keep the enemy off balance. 'Once we allow him to get his breath back', he told Lieutenant-General Birdwood, the commander of I Anzac Corps, 'we shall have to make another of these gigantic assaults...I think our way keeps down casualties and brings the best results.' [7] What this statement appeared to overlook was the fact that limited attacks on narrow fronts permitted the Germans, in most cases, to concentrate much of their available firepower on the threatened sector. Even Haig, who was usually willing to leave the *detailed* planning and conduct of operations to subordinate commanders, reminded them on 2 August that they must practise 'economy of men'. [8] Later the same month, Haig left Rawlinson in little doubt that he was dissatisfied with attacks on narrow fronts by insufficient forces and with inadequate supervision from senior commanders. For the mid-September attack, he stressed, 'a sufficient force must be employed in proper proportion to the extent of front...' [9]

It should be remembered that the Germans were not immune from suffering and that they also committed their fair share of mistakes. In the first two months of the battle the policy of General Erich von Falkenhayn, then Chief of the German General Staff, was that any ground lost should be retaken by immediate counter-attack. The tactical combination of dogged linear defence and incessant counter-attacks which stemmed from this policy sapped the strength of the German Army at a rate no less dramatic than that experienced by the BEF. German units arriving on the Somme from other sectors were soon all too aware that, as British munitions production got into its stride, the Allies were winning the war of matériel. When, on 29 August, Falkenhayn was replaced by Field-Marshal Paul von Hindenburg - with General Erich Ludendorff, as his First Quartermaster-General, being given joint responsibility for all decisions - a fresh tactical doctrine of defence in depth was quickly adopted and work began, in the autumn, on a massive new defensive system, known as the Siegfried Stellung (or Hindenburg Line), twenty-five miles behind the existing front.

The major British set-piece assault which took place on 15 September against the German third position was notable for the first-ever use in battle of a new weapon, the tank. The objectives of the Fourth Army on that day included the German third position in front of Flers and the capture of Gueudecourt, Lesboeufs and Morval. The Canadian Corps, part of the Reserve Army, was to seize Courcelette. In the event, the British XV Corps, helped by four of the tanks assigned to the 41st Division, took Flers and High Wood; Martinpuich and Courcelette were also secured. Advancing about 2,500 yards on a front of 4,500 yards, the British gained, in square miles, roughly twice the amount of ground that they had won on 1 July although it required a renewal of the offensive in the last week of September to seize all the objectives. After a particularly effective preliminary

A pack horse loaded with thigh-length trench waders in muddy terrain near Beaumont Hamel, November 1916. Q 1565

bombardment and creeping barrage on the right, where the divisions of XIV Corps were attacking, Lesboeufs and Morval fell on 25 September and Gueudecourt and Combles followed suit the next day. On Gough's front on 26 September, the Reserve Army – in what became known as the Battle of Thiepval Ridge – undertook its biggest operation to date, attacking from Courcelette to the Schwaben Redoubt. The 18th Division, under Major-General Ivor Maxse, cleared Thiepval itself of Germans by noon on 27 September but again the early impetus was lost. The stubborn defenders of the feared Schwaben Redoubt were not completely forced out until 14 October while the fight for, and around, Regina Trench, on the Canadian Corps sector, dragged on into November.

The question has often been posed as to why Haig, having once more failed to achieve the hoped-for breakthrough, persisted with the offensive after the end of September. Most recent commentators suggest that, fed by optimistic reports from Brigadier-General Charteris, his Chief of Intelligence at General Headquarters (GHQ), Haig firmly, if wrongly, believed that the Germans on the Somme were close to collapse. [10] Writing to Sir William Robertson, the Chief of the Imperial General Staff, on 7 October, Haig argued that the offensive 'must be continued without intermission as long as possible'. He admitted that he could not say how near to breaking-point the enemy actually was, but :

> ...he has undoubtedly gone a long way towards it. Many of his troops have reached, and even passed, it at times during the last few weeks, and though the great difficulties of our advance, and the severity of the German discipline, have enabled the enemy's leaders

German barbed wire in the Beaumont Hamel area, November 1916. Q 1530

September, had stayed comparatively dormant since 1 July. Once the Thiepval ridge was in British possession, Haig wanted Gough to strike hard in this sector. The instructions which GHQ issued on 29 September for the next phase of the offensive called for the Fourth Army to advance towards Warlencourt, Le Transloy and Beaulencourt, while the Reserve Army was to launch a two-pronged attack converging on Miraumont, with one blow being delivered northward from the Thiepval ridge and the other coming eastward from the Beaumont Hamel - Hebuterne front . [14] The provisional date selected for the joint attack was 12 October but, as that month wore on, rain turned the battlefield into a morass. The thick mud and mist added greatly to the problems of infantry and gunners alike. In the words of the official historian, the infantry, 'sometimes wet to the skin and almost exhausted before zero hour, were often

to reorganise resistance afresh after every defeat, this cannot go on indefinitely if constant pressure is maintained. [11]

The reality was that, after their crisis of late September, the Germans rapidly recovered their operational equilibrium. It is also true that, in several respects, the BEF was demonstrating considerable improvements in its tactical thinking by the last quarter of 1916. The creeping barrage - a moving curtain of artillery fire behind which the infantry advanced to their objectives - was becoming standard in the BEF, and divisional commanders such as Maxse, and Major-General R B Stephens of the 5th Division, were beginning to advocate a new platoon organisation, including bombing, Lewis gun and rifle grenadier sections, so that infantry units would be much more self-supporting in firepower during an advance. [12] On the other hand, the Germans had swiftly revised their own defensive tactics by withdrawing their machine-gunners just beyond the normal range of a creeping barrage. The key importance of artillery in the preparation of an assault had been amply revealed by the British advances on 14 July and 25 September, when the preliminary bombardments had been sufficiently intense and concentrated, in terms of weight of shell per yard of trench attacked, to ensure success. [13] Yet, the fact that this formula was not consistently applied in 1916 indicates that its significance had been imperfectly understood by Haig, Rawlinson and Gough.

It was against this strategic and tactical background that the focus of operations shifted partly back to the sector immediately north and south of the Ancre which, except for an abortive attack by the 39th and 49th Divisions towards St Pierre Division on 3

Crown Prince Rupprecht of Bavaria (1869-1955). He commanded the original German Sixth Army in Lorraine in August 1914 and was transferred to the Somme-Flanders area to lead a new Sixth Army during the 'race to the sea' that autumn. He stayed on this part of the Western Front, facing the BEF, for most of the war. One of Germany's ablest military leaders, he was given command, in 1916, of the Army Group which bore his name. Q 45320

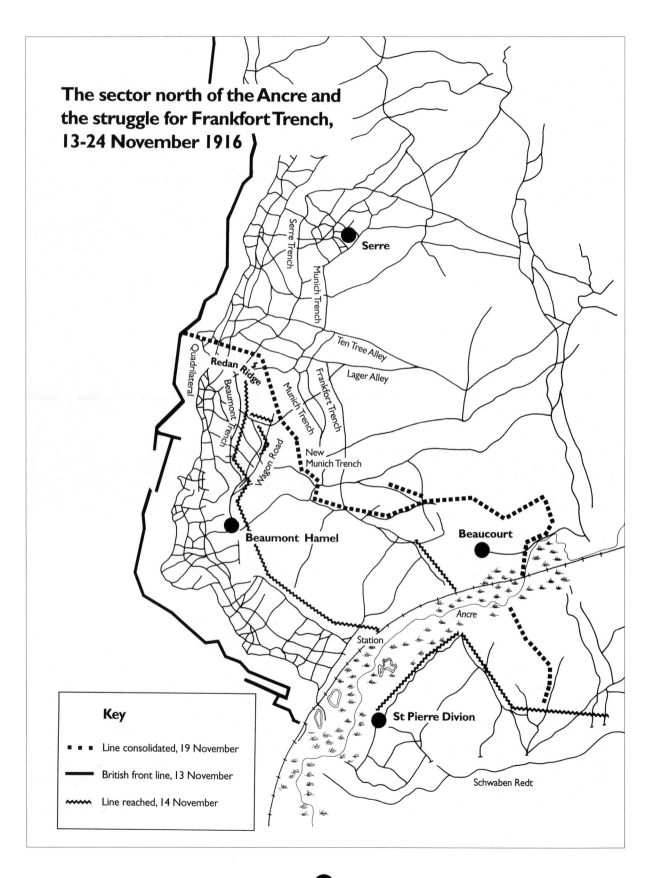

The sector north of the Ancre and the struggle for Frankfort Trench, 13-24 November 1916

Serre Trench

Munich Trench

Serre

Ten Tree Alley

Lager Alley

Quadrilateral

Redan Ridge

Beaumont Trench

Frankfort Trench

Munich Trench

Wagon Road

New Munich Trench

Beaumont Hamel

Beaucourt

Ancre

Station

St Pierre Divion

Schwaben Redt

Key

▪ ▪ ▪ Line consolidated, 19 November

───── British front line, 13 November

⋀⋀⋀ Line reached, 14 November

Bringing in a wounded soldier during the fighting on the Ancre, November 1916. Q 4538

condemned to struggle painfully forward through the mud under heavy fire against objectives vaguely defined and difficult of recognition'. [15]

In the circumstances GHQ was forced to modify its plans and delay Gough's operations on the Ancre. On 17 October, after Haig had consulted Gough and Rawlinson, it was decided that, instead of making a converging advance from both sides of the Ancre valley, the Reserve Army would now attack astride the Ancre, possibly on 23 October, in conjunction with the Fourth Army's efforts to secure Le Transloy. However, the weather remained mostly wet and stormy and, on 3 November, Haig authorised Gough to postpone the Ancre operations indefinitely, so long as arrangements were made to commence the assault without further delay as soon as the weather showed signs of becoming more settled. [16] Five days later, following a visit from Lieutenant-General Sir Launcelot Kiggell, Haig's chief of staff,

Gough conferred with his corps commanders and ruled that, provided no more rain fell, the Fifth Army - as the Reserve Army had now been renamed - would launch its attack on 13 November. [17]

It seems reasonably clear from the evidence that, in the end, it was Gough who was largely responsible for deciding that the Ancre operations should proceed. On the morning of 12 November, when the preliminary bombardment was already in progress, Kiggell visited Gough's headquarters at Toutencourt to ascertain how satisfied the Fifth Army commander was about his chances of success and to underline the fact that Haig did not, in any way, wish to bring on a battle in unfavourable conditions. [18] Gough rated the prospects as 'quite good' and replied that he must either attack on 13 November or withdraw and rest the divisions which were currently in position. In the afternoon Haig himself rode to Toutencourt where Gough, having been to see all the divisions concerned during the day, recommended that the assault should 'go in'. Haig confirmed that a success on the Ancre was highly desirable, not only because it might have a beneficial influence on the Allied situation on the Russian and Rumanian fronts - partly by dissuading the Germans from switching any divisions from France - but also because it would create a favourable impression at the inter-Allied military conference at Chantilly, which Haig was due to attend on 15-16 November. As Haig noted in his diary :

> The British position will doubtless be much stronger (as memories are short) if I could appear there on top of the capture of Beaumont Hamel for instance, and 3,000 German prisoners...But the necessity for a success must not blind eyes to the difficulties of ground and weather. Nothing is so costly as a failure!... [19]

Nevertheless, Haig was reassured by Gough and agreed that the Fifth Army should attack the following day. Writing to the official historian, Sir James Edmonds, after the war, Kiggell observed that 'as things turned out the later stages of the fight were hardly justified, but Gough was so keen and confident the C-in-C decided to permit them'. [20] Another officer, General Sir George Jeffreys - who, as commander of the 57th Brigade in the 19th Division in November 1916, was deeply involved in the Ancre battle - was less circumspect in his criticisms of Gough's misplaced optimism. 'The Army commander and his staff', he recalled, 'had simply no conception of the conditions in the forward area, which were, in fact, about the worst I can remember at any time in the war'. [21]

Considering the obduracy with which the Germans were about to defend the sector, it is perhaps surprising to find that, on the eve of Gough's attack, several senior German officers had grave misgivings regarding their positions on the Ancre. Crown Prince Rupprecht of Bavaria, whose Army Group faced the British on the Somme, was in favour of evacuating the salient between St Pierre Divion and Beaumont Hamel. Ludendorff shared Rupprecht's view and Colonel von Lossberg - the chief of staff to the German First Army and one of the most gifted of all German tacticians - also judged the Serre - Ancre angle to be particularly vulnerable to concentric artillery fire. However, General Fritz von Below, commanding the German First Army, was reluctant to yield high ground which offered his troops valuable observation, so, in practice, the line north of the Ancre was strengthened by the arrival of the

German 12th Division which, from 22 October, took over the Beaumont Hamel sector between the 52nd Division at Serre and the 38th Division at Beaucourt. [22]

In the Fifth Army's attack on 13 November, II Corps (Lieutenant-General C W Jacob), south of the Ancre, was ordered to eject the Germans from the remains of their front system between the Schwaben redoubt and St Pierre Divion and establish a line facing north-east, abreast of Beaucourt. The principal blow was to be delivered north of the Ancre by V Corps (Lieutenant-General E A Fanshawe). Here, from right to left, the 63rd (Royal Naval), 51st (Highland), 2nd and 3rd Divisions were to assault the original German defences between Beaucourt and Serre which had resisted capture on, and since, 1 July 1916. The first objective of V Corps, in what was intended to be a three-stage operation, extended from Beaucourt station on the Ancre, up the Beaumont Hamel valley and around the eastern edge of the village, and then across Redan Ridge and the slope in front of Serre. An average advance of 800 yards would be necessary to complete this stage. 600 to 1,000 yards further on lay the second objective, which ran from the western edge of Beaucourt and along the eastern slope of Redan Ridge before bending around the eastern edge of Serre, where a defensive flank was to be formed. The third corps objective was Beaucourt, on the right near the Ancre. On the part of the front which concerns us most - that of the 51st (Highland) and 2nd Divisions - the objectives included Munich Trench which, in July, had formed an intermediate line between the German front defences and their second position from Grandcourt to Puisieux. Frankfort Trench, the second and final objective of the 51st and 2nd Divisions on 13 November, was 200-400 yards beyond Munich Trench, on the reverse slope of Redan Ridge.

1,401 artillery pieces were available to prepare and support the British assault. In the case of V Corps, they comprised 472 field guns and howitzers and 173 heavy guns and howitzers. This meant that, to support V Corps, there was one field gun to every 13.5 yards and one heavy gun to every 31 yards of front. In comparison, there had been one field gun to every 21 yards and one heavy gun to every 57 yards on 1 July, and one field gun per 10 yards and one heavy gun per 21 yards on 15 September. [23]

The attack, launched in a dank fog at 5.45 am on 13 November, had mixed fortunes. On the II Corps front, the 39th Division, and two battalions of the 19th Division, took most of their initial objectives, including St Pierre Divion, at a cost of under 1,000 casualties. On the other side of the Ancre, the 63rd (Royal Naval) Division -

A wounded British soldier, photographed at a dressing station in Aveluy Wood on 13 November 1916, shows comrades his steel helmet which has been damaged on the first day of Gough's attack astride the Ancre. Q 4510

in its first battle on the Western Front - had a tough fight for Beaucourt, but, with the help of units of the 37th Division, finally secured the village the following morning. The 51st Division cleared the ruins of Beaumont Hamel by the late afternoon of 13 November to give Haig the prize he particularly wanted in time for the Chantilly conference. Unable, for the moment, to push on to the next objective, 250 yards of Frankfort Trench overlooking the Beaucourt valley, the Highlanders paused to consolidate their gains.

Further north the assault was generally less successful. On the left flank, opposite Serre, the troops of the 76th Brigade (3rd Division) were hampered by clinging mud, which was waist deep in places. Finding few gaps in the German wire, they were only able to enter the enemy trenches in small groups. Some of the men of the 8th Brigade, also part of the 3rd Division, crossed the German support and reserve trenches to reach the first objective, Serre Trench, but, again, they were only in isolated parties and were inevitably overpowered. The British 2nd Division, between the 3rd and 51st Divisions, attacked the German positions along Redan Ridge. Its 5th Brigade arrived, on schedule, at its own first objective, Beaumont Trench, which stretched northward from Beaumont Hamel, though the leading troops suffered heavily from rifle and machine-gun fire. The 6th Brigade, on the left, soon ran into difficulties, especially around the Quadrilateral. Mud, intact German wire and enfilade fire from German machine guns all impeded progress. While parties of the 13th Essex Regiment and 1st King's (Liverpool) Regiment pressed on to the first objective near the junction of Beaumont Trench and Lager Alley, most survivors of the leading wave of battalions were held up in the German front trench.

By 7.30 am, when the battalions of the second wave were expected to attack Frankfort Trench, only those of the 5th Brigade were in any position to adhere to the programme and even they could barely muster 120 men from the 17th Royal Fusiliers and the 2nd Oxfordshire and Buckinghamshire Light Infantry. Joined by a handful of men from the 13th Essex and 1st King's of the 6th Brigade, they reached various sections of Frankfort Trench but nowhere in sufficient numbers to hold it. The scattered groups were eventually compelled to fall back, at first to Munich Trench, 200 yards to the west, and then to Wagon Road and Beaumont Trench. At 9.30 am, orders were received from V Corps for a fresh attack in co-operation with the 3rd Division. These orders were cancelled when the 3rd Division's true situation became known and the renewed assault was postponed until the following morning. With Gough still confident that V Corps could capture its original objectives, a formal operation order was issued by that corps to its divisions two hours before midnight. The 51st and 2nd Divisions would once more attempt to carry Frankfort Trench. The Germans, however, used the hours of darkness to reinforce their troops on the Ancre, parts of the 26th Reserve and 223rd Divisions moving up to support the 12th Division north of the river. Of these formations, the 12th and 26th Reserve Divisions had already fought, and suffered severe casualties, on the Somme during the summer. The 223rd Division was a new formation but it comprised regiments which had previously seen service at Verdun and in Lorraine. All three were regarded by the Allies as good divisions. [24]

It was frequently the case in 1916 that, once the set-piece phase of a British assault was over and the early momentum was lost, subsequent attacks became piecemeal, hastily-organised affairs which lacked both weight and co-ordination. The efforts of V Corps to seize Munich and Frankfort Trenches on the morning of 14 November followed this depressingly familiar pattern. The 51st Division's 152nd Brigade was meant to attack Munich Trench at 6.20 am, at the same time as the 2nd Division, but the attached 1/7th Argyll and Sutherland Highlanders received their orders late and could do little other than to send forward strong patrols against stubborn opposition. A two-company advance at 7.30 am secured the southern portion of Munich Trench after about an hour, the troops observing that Frankfort Trench appeared to be bristling with Germans. Before any further advance could be attempted, Munich Trench was shelled in error by a British heavy battery and the Highlanders were forced to withdraw some distance.

The 2nd Division at least started its attack on time at 6.20 am, using two battalions of the 99th Brigade from divisional reserve. An erratic supporting barrage caused many casualties and, being new to the ground, some troops lost direction. The 1st King's Royal Rifle Corps on the right were stopped short of the objective and ultimately retired to Wagon Road, though with 60 prisoners. The 1st Royal Berkshire Regiment got as far as Munich Trench but in insufficient numbers to effect a permanent lodgement, likewise dropping back to Wagon Road during the morning. The one bright spot of the morning for the British was the fact that the barrage covering the left of the assault broke up a German counter-attack from Serre while the 22nd Royal Fusiliers came up to strengthen the 2nd Division's positions on this flank. [25]

Undeterred by the events of the early morning, V Corps ordered a resumption of the attack on Frankfort Trench by the 2nd and 51st Divisions at 2.45 pm. As before, the orders reached the Highlanders too late, leaving two battalions of the 112th Brigade (37th Division) - lent to the 2nd Division for the purpose - to attack alone. It was a measure of the poor communications on the battlefield that the divisional headquarters did not know that the previous attack on Munich Trench had failed. Consequently, when the 11th Royal Warwickshires and 6th Bedfordshires advanced, after an exhausting approach march, they ran into unexpected machine-gun fire from that quarter and could do no more than add to the congestion of units along the sunken Wagon Road. Most of the available German troops in the Munich-Frankfort position had been needed to halt the attack and British artillery fire had prevented them from being re-supplied with bombs (grenades) and small arms ammunition, although part of the German 208th Division, following a two-month spell on the Eastern Front, began to relieve the hard-pressed 12th Division. That night, on the British side of No Man's Land, Pioneers and Royal Engineers of the 51st Division hurriedly dug a new line, called 'New Munich Trench', about 200 yards west of Munich Trench itself. [26]

Fanshawe, the V Corps commander, had been visited by Gough at noon on 14 November. With Gough's consent, orders were issued for a general resumption of the attack the next day. Apparently ignorant of the fact that Munich Trench was still occupied by the Germans, V Corps ordered the 2nd and 51st Divisions to mount a fresh assault towards Frankfort Trench at 9am on 15 November. During the evening of 14 November, Haig, who was now in Paris, learned of Gough's plans for the morrow and immediately telephoned GHQ to indicate that he did not want the Fifth Army to embark upon any more large-scale operations before he returned from Chantilly. [27] Kiggell went to see Gough at 9am on 15 November to make sure that Haig's views about the resumption of the offensive were not lost on the Fifth Army commander. [28] Even as the two officers met, however, the joint attack by the 2nd and 51st Divisions was being delivered.

Many of the ingredients common to hastily-prepared minor operations and follow-up attacks were evident in the assault of 15 November and, predictably, they again combined to produce a recipe for failure. The 1/7th Argyll and Sutherland Highlanders advanced from New Munich Trench, about 500 yards further forward than the jumping-off positions of the 2nd Division in Beaumont Trench, and, partly as a result of this difference in alignment, ran into their own barrage. Some Highlanders reached Frankfort Trench and lobbed bombs into dugouts but, being outnumbered, withdrew to their starting-point, covered by Lewis guns. The 2nd Division employed two more battalions - the 8th East Lancashires and 10th Loyal North Lancashires - from the attached 112th Brigade (37th Division) and these units did not arrive at their assembly trenches until forty minutes before zero hour. Major-General W G Walker, commander of the 2nd Division, had tried in vain to persuade V Corps to postpone the attack until 1pm to allow these troops time for reconnaissance. Not surprisingly, when their assault was made, the Lancashire battalions soon lost direction and, having sustained heavy casualties in officers, withdrew to Wagon Road like several units before them in the past fifty or so hours.

After Kiggell's visit on the morning of 15 November, Gough met his corps commanders, Jacob and Fanshawe, and subsequently telephoned GHQ to tell Kiggell that all were agreed that a resumption of the Ancre attack had good prospects of success. Pointing out that further gains would improve the Fifth Army's line, he proposed two more days of offensive operations, beginning on 17 November, if Haig was willing to let him proceed. Gough was certainly overstating his case in claiming that 'all ranks were keen to attack again', for, as George Jeffreys later asserted, 'he had no notion of the physical strain on the troops of even a few hours in the line under such conditions'. Nevertheless, when Kiggell discussed the situation with Haig in Paris that evening, Gough's proposals were approved. To be fair to Gough, even his seemingly unshakeable optimism was dented by the failures of 15 November. Meeting Jacob and Fanshawe again on 16 November, he admitted that, although Munich and Frankfort Trenches had yet to be captured, the Fifth Army had already used up more men

Graves in New Munich Trench British Cemetery, November 1992. The spire of Beaumont Hamel church, to the west, is just visible in the middle distance. Photograph by Chris McCarthy

than anticipated ; it was doubtful if enough troops could be assembled to launch a further attack on Serre, and Grandcourt too might be out of reach. While V Corps still had the task of seizing Frankfort Trench, the main role in the next attack was now allotted to II Corps, south of the Ancre, where it was to advance 500 yards towards Grandcourt Trench, secure a line south of Grandcourt and push forward to the western edge of the village. [29]

At this juncture the British 32nd Division, under Major-General W H Rycroft, was transferred from the II Corps reserve to V Corps, and came up to relieve troops of the 2nd and 51st Divisions, these formations having incurred some 3,000 and 2,200 casualties respectively in the fighting since 13 November. Seven of the 32nd Division's twelve infantry battalions were locally-raised or 'Pals' battalions.' They included three battalions raised in Glasgow : the 15th Highland Light Infantry (HLI), originally recruited from the city's Tramways Department; the 16th HLI, recruited largely from current and former members of the local Boys' Brigade; and the 17th HLI, raised by the Glasgow Chamber of Commerce from students and ex-pupils of the Glasgow Academy,

Royal Glasgow Technical College and various high schools as well as from the city's business houses and offices. [30] The 16th Northumberland Fusiliers (Newcastle Commercials) contained many volunteers from businesses on the Newcastle Quayside, whilst the 15th and 16th Lancashire Fusiliers had been raised in and around Salford by a committee headed by Montague Barlow MP. [31] The 11th Battalion of the Border Regiment - known as the 'Lonsdales' - had been recruited by the Earl of Lonsdale and an executive committee in Cumberland and Westmorland. [32] The remaining infantry formations in the division were mostly Regular units, except for an amalgamated Territorial battalion, the 5/6th Royal Scots, formed from two units which had served on Gallipoli. This battalion had joined the division on 29 July 1916. [33]

The 32nd Division had fought bravely at Thiepval from 1 to 3 July, suffering 4,676 casualties. Its 97th Brigade, deployed in No Man's Land before zero hour on 1 July, took and held the Leipzig Redoubt at the tip of the Leipzig Salient but, apart from this brilliant feat, the division had largely failed to secure its objectives in the opening days of the offensive. It had later participated in attempts to complete the capture of Ovillers between 13 and 15 July before moving north for three months of routine trench warfare in the Cambrin, Hulluch and Cuinchy sectors near Bethune. Despite their losses in July, and the subsequent changes to the Army's reserve and drafting system which meant that reinforcements and casualty replacements no longer necessarily came from a unit's parent regiment or recruiting area, most of the division's Pals battalions still contained a small nucleus of their original members. [34]

There is evidence to suggest that all was not well in the command and staff echelons of the division. Austin Girdwood, who was a GS02 on the staff of the division in July and commanded the Lonsdales in November 1916, accused Rycroft, a cavalryman, of being ignorant about, and unsympathetic towards, the infantry. [35] Girdwood complained, in particular, that before 1 July Rycroft had exhausted the infantry by keeping them in the line too long and using too many of them on working parties. 'Naturally I got myself disliked', wrote Girdwood, 'and the proof is in the fact that...I was given command of a Battalion to get me out of the Staff Office'. [36] Lieutenant-Colonel E G Wace, the division's GSOl from 2 May to 28 November, remarked that Gough had been 'furious' with the 32nd Division after its failure at Thiepval and that Rycroft was terrified of the Fifth Army commander:

...Rycroft knew he'd 'got it in for us', and when at Bethune we got orders to go back to

View from New Munich Trench British Cemetery, looking north to Frankfurt Trench British Cemetery, November 1992. Photograph by Chris McCarthy

the Somme in October he turned to me and said wryly that this would be his undoing unless we went to Rawly's Army ! So he just hadn't the kick in him to stand up to Gough, when all initiative was taken out of his hands. [37]

It should be added that at least one battalion commander, Lieutenant-Colonel E J N Davis of the 15th HLI, maintained that Rycroft always gave him 'a feeling of confidence and fair play'. [38]

Rycroft seems to have summoned up enough resolve on 16 November to argue that it would be practically impossible for his division to attack the next day since the line had not been properly reconnoitred and forming-up positions had not been marked out. [39] The attack was put back until 6.10 am on 18 November but this was by no means the sole problem facing the 32nd Division. Both Wace and Davis asserted that the GSOl and some battalion officers of the 2nd Division, when being relieved, could not give them correct positional 'fixes' for the front line or their own headquarters. Davis found that the 15th HLI were consequently 300 yards or more south of the sub-sector they were supposed to have taken over, a factor which had serious implications for the accuracy of the covering barrage on the day of the assault . [40] To make matters worse, the 32nd Division's own artillery was elsewhere in the line, having been assisting the 51st Division, so much of the assault on 18 November would be covered by gunners of the 2nd Division. 'In this way', wrote one of the 32nd Division's artillery brigade commanders, 'the mutual confidence and knowledge of each other was wasted'. [41]

The ground itself - pitted as it was with shell holes from the recent fighting - also militated against rapid movement or re-supply in the front line area. An officer who served on the staff of the 14th Brigade in November 1916 went so far as to say that 'the climatic conditions alone made it clear from the start to the very stupidest brain that no success could possibly result'. [42] The 2nd Manchesters, part of that brigade, 'were so overdone with working parties and fatigues that they were not too fit for the attack when it came...' [43] But, even with the extra day, the division's principal problem was the lack of time allowed for preparation. The Fifth Army operation order for the attack was issued at 8pm on 16 November and the 32nd Division's own operation order at 3.45 pm the following day, although the latter appears to have reached the 14th Brigade headquarters, for example, too late to enable the brigade staff to issue their own orders until 11.30pm on 17 November, less than seven hours before the attack. Because of the difficulties of communication in the forward area, some of these orders did not reach assaulting battalions until 4.30 am on the morning of the attack. Units on their way to the line became lost and only ten minutes remained before zero hour when the last of the 16th HLI's attacking troops arrived, half-frozen and exhausted, in their jumping-off positions, having had no hot food for fifteen hours. [44]

The assault at 6.10 am was launched in sleet and snow, which later turned to rain. The conditions underfoot became extremely slippery while the problems facing the gunners - who were already hampered by poor visibility - were compounded by the intense cold, which affected the shell fuzes and made an accurate barrage even more difficult to achieve. [45] On the left, the 14th Brigade attacked with two battalions, the 2nd Manchesters and the 15th HLI, to carry the defensive flank forward some 500 yards to the line of Ten Tree Alley. The 97th Brigade was ordered by V Corps to use all its four infantry battalions in the attack on Munich and Frankfort Trenches, a decision which appears to have been influenced by Gough himself. The order greatly reduced Rycroft's options if things went wrong, although it had the virtue of giving added weight to the assault. [46]

As their commanding officer had feared, the 15th HLI, the left-hand battalion of the 14th Brigade, received negligible help from the covering barrage, which fell up to 600 yards too far ahead. The troops endeavoured to bomb their way forward and made slight gains on the left, near the Quadrilateral, but further progress was blocked by close-range machine-gun fire. [47] The 2nd Manchesters, unable, in the time available, to dig forming-up trenches, pushed eastward along Lager Alley before zero hour and, when the overall attack was delivered, advanced down into the valley in the direction of Serre. A few small groups even reached that village

Looking north along Redan Ridge, towards Ten Tree Alley and Serre, near the original site of Frankfort Trench, November 1992. Photograph by Chris McCarthy

where, with ammunition supplies running out, they were overwhelmed, during the afternoon, by a counter-attack involving elements of the German 52nd and 223rd Divisions. Nothing was subsequently heard from the three leading companies of the 2nd Manchesters. [48]

The British barrage was similarly erratic on the 97th Brigade's front. When it opened, it was particularly short on the right, killing and wounding many men of the 17th HLI who were lying out in front of New Munich Trench prior to the assault. The Germans, manning Munich Trench in some force, were relatively untouched by the ragged barrage and stopped the 17th HLI's attack with rifle and machine-gun fire, driving the survivors back on New Munich Trench. [49] The right-hand company of the 16th HLI – 'A' Company - which was next in line, shared the same fate. However, on the 16th HLI's left, the barrage was much better and three platoons of 'D' Company not only stormed across Munich Trench but also took and held a portion of Frankfort Trench, the final objective. The 11th Border Regiment was another battalion which suffered the consequences of supporting artillery fire that fell short. 'To say that the British barrage was ineffective is too mild altogether', wrote the commanding officer of the Lonsdales. In spite of this bad start, parties of the Lonsdales succeeded in joining the group from the 16th HLI in Frankfort Trench. The 2nd King's Own Yorkshire Light Infantry (KOYLI), on the 97th Brigade's left flank, could not render any real assistance in the crucial sector, its own right-hand companies being held up by a strongpoint in Munich Trench. German retention of Munich Trench condemned the 97th Brigade's attack to failure. The remainder of the 16th HLI and the Lonsdales withdrew to Wagon Road following a German counter-attack, leaving their comrades cut off, behind German lines, in Frankfort Trench. [50]

Some German units in the Redan Ridge area, such as the 62nd Infantry Regiment (12th Division), were now down to a fraction of their former strength. Rycroft wished to bring up battalions of his divisional reserve, the 96th Brigade, at dusk for a further attack against Munich Trench. The corps commander agreed but the plan was vetoed by Gough's headquarters. [51] In fact, given the conditions and its casualties, it is doubtful whether the 32nd Division was capable of another major assault so soon. The 16th HLI alone, for example, had lost thirteen officers and 390 NCOs and men killed, wounded and missing on 18 November and, as a staff officer of the 14th Brigade remembered, this was 'the only occasion on which I saw men dead from exhaustion from their efforts to get out of the mud'. [52] The division's post-battle analysis argued, however, that if Brigadier-General J B Jardine's 97th Brigade had not been obliged to attack with all four battalions at zero hour on 18 November, and had been permitted to keep troops in hand to give the assault more depth and exploit any early success, then the Germans might have been driven out of their positions. [53]

Estimates vary as to the size of the party which remained isolated in Frankfort Trench, although the most detailed contemporary reports put it at seven officers and just over 120 other ranks, including three officers and 60 other ranks from the 16th HLI, the same number of officers and men from the 11th Border Regiment, and one officer and three other ranks from the 2nd KOYLI. Of these, between 30 and 50 were wounded, some seriously. [54] The tiny garrison occupied two dugouts in the captured portion of trench, one being allocated to the wounded and the other to those still fit to fight. They had four Lewis guns and a limited quantity of ammunition, which they supplemented by taking what they could from the dead lying in the open. Most men handed over their small arms ammunition to the Lewis gunners and armed themselves with German rifles and cartridges. Bombs were scarce and there was very little food and water. Many of the men had already consumed their water and iron rations. Again, the dead were searched at night for additional rations, while water was collected from shell holes and boiled over improvised lamps, using rifle oil as fuel and fragments of cleaning flannel as wicks. [55]

On 19 November, as the 97th Brigade was relieved by the 96th Brigade along Wagon Road and New Munich Trench, the British troops in Frankfort Trench consolidated their defences, placed their machine guns at vital points and organised a system of sentry duties, the Germans, at this stage, apparently being unaware of their presence. This state of affairs did not last much longer for, on 20 November, the third day of the isolated garrison's ordeal, a strong German raiding party moved across the open and bombed the captured portion of Frankfort Trench on the right. Beaten off with rifles, machine guns and bombs, the Germans retired, leaving behind many casualties. Heartening as this action was to the dogged defenders, they too had incurred more losses, compelling them to evacuate the smaller of the two dugouts and to shorten their line to economise on manpower. [56] Half an hour before midnight, two members of the beleaguered garrison - Company Sergeant-Major Johnstone and Private Dixon of the 11th Borders - crawled out of Frankfort Trench and, guided by a bright star and the occasional illumination afforded by Very lights, evaded the German sentries and working parties and reached the 96th Brigade's lines in the early hours of 21 November. [57]

As the fourth day of the siege of Frankfort Trench dawned, the garrison's plight was becoming desperate. The men were now weakened by hunger and an almost unbearable thirst. Many of the wounds were turning gangrenous but there was no water available to wash bandages, nor drugs to ease the pain. Hopes rose, however, when a signaller managed to attract the attention of a British pilot by using pieces of a torn shirt. Several more aircraft appeared after an interval to flash the message that relief was on the way. Two soldiers of the 16th HLI, in particular, displayed outstanding leadership during this phase of the siege. One was Company Sergeant-Major George Lee, a roads foreman with Glasgow Corporation in civilian life, who was subsequently described as 'the heart and soul of the defence'. The other was Lance-Corporal John Veitch, the son of a sergeant in the Scots Greys, who played a key role in the deployment and handling of the Lewis guns in the captured trench. Neither survived the battle but both earned a posthumous mention in despatches. [58]

When the first definite news of the situation of the isolated party had reached the 32nd Division's headquarters, it had been decided to send out, on the night of 21-22 November, a party of two officers and 60 men - drawn equally from the Lonsdales and the 16th HLI - in an attempt to rescue their stranded comrades. The party was to be guided by Company Sergeant-Major Johnstone, who had escaped from Frankfort Trench the previous night. The relief party left Wagon Road at 9.30 pm and arrived at the German wire in front of Munich Trench about seventy-five minutes later. Johnstone then worked his way along the wire to the south and the north, but the night was very dark and there was also a ground mist and he was unable to find a suitable gap through which the patrol might pass in order to cross Munich Trench. The officer in command therefore withdrew the party to Wagon Road, which was reached at 2.25 am. By this time, Haig had told Gough that Rycroft was unfit to command a division and that his brigadiers 'had not been taught anything by him'. Brigadier-General R W R Barnes of the 111th Brigade, 37th Division, was chosen by Haig as Rycroft's successor, one of his earliest acts on 22 November being to report to V Corps on the previous night's attempt to relieve Frankfort Trench. His conclusion was that Company Sergeant-Major Johnstone had exaggerated the extent to which the German wire represented an obstacle, though Barnes did admit, somewhat condescendingly, that Johnstone 'had gone through a very trying 24 hours and was probably feeling the strain of it'. [59]

According to the published battalion history of the 16th HLI, the Germans launched a powerful attack from both the front and flanks against the dwindling British band in Frankfort Trench on the afternoon of the sixth day, 23 November. The weary defenders somehow mustered the strength and courage to beat back the Germans, even taking eight prisoners in a fierce fight at close quarters. [60]

At 11pm on 21 November - while Johnstone was still trying to find a way through the German wire and two more men, a lance-corporal and a private, were escaping from Frankfort Trench - Fanshawe, the corps commander, had held a conference at which it was decided to make another effort to relieve the marooned party. The operation was to be undertaken by three companies of the 16th Lancashire Fusiliers and one company of the 2nd Royal Inniskilling Fusiliers, all from the 96th Brigade, attacking in four waves. The second wave was given the vital task of passing over the initial objective - Munich Trench - and pressing on to rescue the Frankfort Trench garrison. Reports from officers who reconnoitred the German wire on the night of 22-23 November revealed that Johnstone had, in fact, been right and that the wire in front of Munich Trench was relatively intact. The artillery were therefore directed to begin wire cutting as soon as possible on 23 November. Shortly before noon, divisional headquarters fixed zero hour for 3.30pm.

The 96th Brigade's attack on 23 November began well. Keeping close to the covering barrage, the troops reached Munich Trench with little opposition but, because of the nature of the ground and the remains of the German wire, they did not reach the objective

simultaneously at all points. This early loss of cohesion notwithstanding, the men of the first wave jumped into Munich Trench as they arrived to deal with the German garrison there. The second wave crossed Munich Trench as ordered and pushed on until they ran into their own barrage. Pausing to reorganise, they resumed their advance although all the officers and NCOs were killed or wounded as they encountered heavy machine-gun fire from a trench on the right which had not been subdued by the British artillery. The survivors of the second wave were forced back to Munich Trench where, because some portions of the objective had not been immediately secured, the Germans had been able to emerge from dugouts to engage their attackers in bombing duels. The fight continued until about 4.20 pm when the British were at last compelled to retire, suffering further casualties as they did so from machine guns on both flanks. In total the 96th Brigade lost seven officers and 224 other ranks - over 60 per cent of those taking part in the operation. [61]

The failure of the 96th Brigade's attack removed any lingering hopes that the Frankfort Trench garrison might be saved. During the night of 23-24 November, the 7th Division began to relieve the 32nd Division, which left the sector having suffered 2,524 casualties in six days, a large proportion of these having been posted as missing. [62] On the seventh day of the siege of Frankfort Trench, the Germans, under cover of a white flag, sent a message calling upon the garrison to surrender. When, after due consideration, the request was ignored, the Germans shelled the trench heavily, killing Company Sergeant-Major Lee among others. On 25 November the Germans delivered an attack in force from all points of the compass. There could only be one outcome. The tiny garrison was finally overwhelmed and the survivors taken prisoner. Only fifteen of the original number were left unwounded and even they were so weak that they could scarcely stand. [63]

The Somme offensive was now over. It had cost the BEF 419,654 casualties for a strip of territory approximately six miles deep by twenty miles wide. Although Beaumont Hamel and Beaucourt had fallen, the Germans had stopped Gough's attempt to secure the Munich-Frankfort position on Redan Ridge in the last phase of the battle. The capture of Munich Trench by the 7th Division on 11 January 1917 made it possible to clear the crest of the Beaumont Hamel spur in the second half of that month, but Serre was held by the Germans until they abandoned the sector on 24 February, during the preliminary stages of their withdrawal to the Hindenburg Line.

The gallantry of the 32nd Division was eventually acknowledged by the award, after the Armistice, of a large number of decorations to the survivors of Frankfort Trench - an unusual step, in that it was comparatively rare to confer decorations upon prisoners of war. To his credit, Gough warmly endorsed the recommendations, stating that the attack on 18 November had demanded considerable 'grit and courage' and that the feat of the Frankfort Trench garrison deserved recognition as a 'magnificent example of soldierly qualities'. [64] Indeed, the achievement of the front-line troops of the division in storming and holding Frankfort Trench, given all the disadvantages arising from poor planning and appalling conditions, demonstrated just how good the raw material of the New Armies actually was in 1916. Responsibility for the sacrifice of the best part of two divisions for a limited objective lies elsewhere. Gough must bear the brunt of the overall blame for persisting with hurriedly-planned and badly-co-ordinated small-scale operations after the capture of Beaumont Hamel on 13 November. His performance at Bullecourt in April-May 1917 and at Langemarck during the Third Battle of Ypres in August that year suggests that he had learned little from the experience of the Ancre either in terms of curbing his natural impetuosity or in the art of planning and conducting operations in bad conditions. Gough, a friend of Haig, survived the setbacks of 1916 and 1917 whereas, in addition to Rycroft, the GSO1 of the 32nd Division

(Lieutenant-Colonel Wace) and two brigade commanders - Compton of 14th Brigade and Yatman of 96th Brigade - were removed in the week following the Ancre battle. If this clear-out of senior officers was perhaps a trifle unfair and drastic, there is no doubt that bad staff work contributed to the division's failure. As Austin Girdwood later wrote:

> I know what the same units could do when the Division was commanded by a man like 'Tiger' Shute who worked us hard but sensibly and who damned us all to heaps but whom we all adored all the same because he understood infantry...He had Macnamara [sic] and Lumsden to back him up and that is why the Division did so brilliantly afterwards. [65]

Recent studies have argued convincingly that the BEF on the Western Front *did* show a progressive improvement - albeit with some hiccups - in its offensive tactics and performance between 1916 and the Armistice. [66] By August 1918, for example, changes in the organisation of infantry platoons and also the considerable refinement of gunnery tactics and techniques, enabled British and Dominion divisions to maintain the momentum of an advance, beyond the assault phase, to a much greater extent than they had in the past. However painful it had been, the experience gained on the Somme in 1916 was an important and necessary part of that 'learning curve'.

Notes

1. The alternative spelling 'Frankfurt Trench' is also used in a variety of sources, and the small cemetery still located near the scene of the 32nd Division's attack is called 'Frankfort Trench British Cemetery'. However, in this article, I have employed the spelling 'Frankfort Trench' which is given in the British official history and the majority of contemporary documents.
2. See footnote 2 on pages 522-3 of Captain Wilfrid Miles, *Military Operations: France and Belgium, 1916,* Volume 2, Macmillan, London, 1938.
3. Haig was promoted to field-marshal at the beginning of 1917 .
4. Two particularly stimulating and scholarly recent studies of the BEF's part in the Battle of the Somme can be found in Tim Travers, *The Killing Ground : The British Army, the Western*

Front and the Emergence of Modern Warfare, 1900- 1918, Allen and Unwin, London, 1987, pp. 127-199 , and Robin Prior and Trevor Wilson, *Command on the Western Front: The Military Career of Sir Henry Rawlinson, 1914-18,* Blackwell, Oxford, 1992 pp 137-260.
5. Gerard J De Groot, *Douglas Haig, 1861-1928,* Unwin Hyman, London, 1988, pp 260-3 ; Travers, *The Killing Ground,* pp 173-7; Miles, *Military Operations,* 1900, Vol 2, pp 174-5.
6. Prior and Wilson, *Command on the Western Front,* pp 203-5.
7. Anthony Farrar-Hockley, *Goughie : The Life of General Sir Hubert Gough,* Hart-Davis, MacGibbon, London, 1975, p 190.
8. 'The Commander-in-Chief's Instructions to the Fourth and Reserve Armies, 2nd August' (OAD 91), 2 August 1916, given in *Military Operations: France and Belgium, 1916,*

Maps and Appendices volume, Appendix 13, pp 34-6.
9. General Headquarters (GHQ) to Fourth Army (OAD 123), 24th August 1916, Fourth Army papers, Vol 5, IWM.
10. See, for instance, Travers, T*he Killing Ground,* pp 183-7 and De Groot, *Douglas Haig,* pp 269-71.
11. Haig to CIGS (Robertson), 'Present Situation' (OAD 173), 7 October 1916, PRO WO 158/21.
12. Shelford Bidwell and Dominick Graham, *Firepower : British Army Weapons and Theories of War, 1904-45,* Allen and Unwin, London, 1982, pp 120-1 ; see also Bill Rawling, *Surviving Trench Warfare : Technology and the Canadian Corps, 1914-1918,* University of Toronto Press, 1992, pp 83-6.
13. Prior and Wilson, *Command on the Western Front,* pp 197, 233-7, 249.
14. Miles, *Military Operations,* Vol 2, pp 391-3, 427-8.

15. Ibid, p 458.
16. Ibid, pp 458-9, 461-2.
17. Ibid, p 462.
18. Ibid, p 476.
19. Haig Diary, 12 November 1916, PRO WO 256/14. I am most grateful to the present Earl Haig for kindly granting me permission to include this and other quotations from his father's diary.
20. Kiggell to Edmonds, 4 June 1938, PRO CAB 45/135.
21. Jeffreys to Edmonds, 23 October 1936, PRO CAB 45/135.
22. Miles, *Military Operations, 1916,* Vol 2, Note II, P 475.
23. Ibid., p 478, footnote 1.
24. *Histories of Two Hundred and Fifty-One Divisions of the German Army Which Participated in the War (1914-1918),* United States War Department, 1920, see London Stamp Exchange edition, 1989, pp 211-14, 365-8, 702-4 ; Miles, op cit., p 503.

25. One of those who fell on 14 November was Lance-Sergeant Hector Munro of the 22nd (Service) Battalion, Royal Fusiliers (Kensington). Munro was better known as the author and satirist 'Saki'. See G D Sheffield and G I S Inglis (eds.), *From Vimy Ridge to the Rhine : the Great War Letters of Christopher Stone, DSO MC*, Crowood Press, Marlborough, 1989, pp 14, 19, 75 ; also A J Langguth, *Saki : A Life of Hector Hugh Munro*, Oxford University Press, 1981 ; Miles, op cit, pp 506-8.

26. Paul Fiedel, *Geschichte des Infanterie-Regiments von Winterfeldt (2. Oberschlesisches) Nr.23 : Das Regiment im Weltkriege*, Berlin, 1929, pp 150-63.

27. Miles, op. cit., pp 507-8.

28. Ibid., p 511.

29. Jeffreys to Edmonds, 23 October 1936, PRO CAB 45/135 ; Miles, op cit, pp 511-12.

30. Thomas Chalmers (ed.), *An Epic of Glasgow ; History of the 15th Battalion the Highland Light Infantry (City of Glasgow Regiment)*, McCallum, Glasgow, 1934, p 2 ; also *A Saga of Scotland : History of the 16th Battalion the Highland Light Infantry*, McCallum, Glasgow, 1930, pp 1-3 ; J W Arthur and I S Munro (ed), *The Seventeenth Highland Light Infantry (Glasgow Chamber of Commerce Battalion) Record of War Service, 1914-1918*, Clark, Glasgow, 1920, pp 14-15.

31. Captain C H Cooke, *Historical Records of the 16th (Service) Battalion Northumberland Fusiliers*, Newcastle and Gateshead Chamber of Commerce, 1923, pp 1-2 ; Sir C A Montague Barlow (ed.), *The Lancashire Fusiliers : The Roll of Honour of the Salford Brigade*, Sherratt and Hughes, Manchester, 1920, pp 23-30.

32. 'V M', *Record of the XIth (Service) Battalion Border Regiment (Lonsdale) from September 1914 to July 1st 1916*, Whitehead, Appleby, n d, p 6. Hugh Cecil Lowther, the fifth Earl of Lonsdale (1857-1944), popularly known as the 'yellow Earl', is perhaps best remembered for his association with the Lonsdale Belt awarded to boxing champions.

33. Major A F Becke, *History of the Great War : Order of Battle of Divisions, Part 3B*, HMSO, London, 1945, pp 21-9.

34. This can be deduced by analysing the personal details contained in the appropriate parts of *Soldiers Died in the Great War, 1914-19*, and in various cemetery registers of the Commonwealth War Graves Commission.

35. GS02 denoted 'General Staff Officer 2nd Grade', and GSO1 stood for 'General Staff Officer 1st Grade'. The 'G' Branch of the General Staff was concerned with such matters as operations, training and military intelligence; the 'A' (Adjutant-General's) Branch dealt with administration, personnel and discipline ; and the 'Q' (Quartermaster-General's) Branch covered such duties as quartering, supply and transportation.

36. Girdwood to Edmonds, 30 June 1930, PRO CAB 45/134.

37. E G Wace to Edmonds, 30 October 1936, PRO CAB 45/138.

38. H J N Davis to Edmonds, 10 November 1936, PRO CAB 45/133.

39. 32nd Division, General Staff: War Diary, July 1916 – February 1917: File marked 'General Ryecroft [sic], Private Diary', entry for 16 November 1916, PRO WO 95/2368.

40. E G Wace to Edmonds, 30 October 1936, PRO CAB 45/138 ; H J N Davis to Edmonds, 10 November 1936, PRO CAB 45/133.

41. R Fitzmaurice to Edmonds, 7 November 1936, PRO CAB 45/133.

42. Leonard Kentish to Edmonds, 19 November 1936, PRO CAB 45/135. See also 17th Battalion, Highland Light Infantry, War Diary, November 1916, PRO WO 95/2403 ; and Major-General R W R Barnes (GOC 32nd Division from 22 November 1916 to 29 January 1917), 'Summary of Operations for week ending 24/11/16', PRO WO 95/2368.

43. N Luxmoore to Edmonds, 2 November 1936, PRO CAB 45/135.

44. Miles, op cit, p. 512 ; 32nd Division Operation Order No.65, 17 November 1916, PRO WO 95/2368 ; Brigadier-General W W Seymour (GOC 14th Brigade, 24 November 1916 to 12 April 1917), Report on 'recent operations' to 32nd Division, 3 December 1916, PRO WO 95/2368; 16th Battalion, Highland Light Infantry : War Diary, November 1916, PRO WO 95/2403 ; Chalmers, *A Saga of Scotland*, pp 50-2.

45. 32nd Division, General Staff: War Diary, July 1916 – February 1917: File marked 'General Ryecroft [sic], Private Diary', Note 'B', PRO WO 95/2368.

46. Wace to Edmonds, 30 October 1936, PRO CAB 45/138 ; Miles, op cit, p 521.

47. H J N Davis to Edmonds, 10 November 1936, PRO CAB 45/133 ; 'Narrative of Operations carried out by 32nd Division, 18 November 1916', PRO WO 95/2368 ; Miles, op cit, p522.

48. 32nd Division, 'Narrative of Operations..., 18 November 1916',

PRO WO 95/2368 ; Major-General W H Rycroft, Report to V Corps, 21 November 1916, PRO WO 95/2368 ; Miles, op cit, p 522 ; Kurt Mucke, *Das Grossherzoglich Badische Infanterie-Regiment Nr.185*, Berlin, 1922, pp 38-42.

49. 17th Battalion, Highland Light Infantry : War Diary, Novenber 1916, PRO WO 95/2403 ; 32nd Division, 'Narrative of Operations..., 18 November 1916', PRO WO 95/2368 ; Rycroft, Report to V Corps, 21 November 1916, PRO WO 95/2368.

50. 16th HLI : War Diary, November 1916, PRO WO 95/2403 ; 11th Battalion, Border Regiment : War Diary, November 1916, PRO WO 95/2403 ; 32nd Division, 'Narrative of Operations...', PRO WO 95/2368; Rycroft, 'Private Diary', entries for 18 and 19 November 1916, and Report to V Corps, 21 November 1916, both PRO WO 95/2368; R Fitzmaurice to Edmonds, 7 November 1936, PRO CAB 45/133; Girdwood to Edmonds, n d, probably 1936, PRO CAB 45/134; Chalmers, *A Saga of Scotland*, pp 52-4.

51. H Reymann, *Das 3 Oberschlesische Infanterie-Regiment Nr. 62 im Kriege 1914-1918*, Zeulenrode, 1930, pp 133-41; Rycroft, 'Private Diary', entry for 18 November 1916, PRO WO 95/2368.

52. 16th HLI : War Diary, November 1916, PRO WO 95/2403 ; Leonard Kentish to Edmonds, 19 November 1936, PRO CAB 45/135.

53. 'Lessons derived from the experiences of 32nd Division in the recent Operations', November 1916, PRO WO 95/2368.

54. 'Report by Majar [R] Rowan on the situation of a party of the 97th Inf. Bde. in the Frankfort Trench', 21 November 1916 ; 32nd Division, 'Narrative of Operations' ; 'Report on Operations carried out by the 32nd Division from Nov. 19th to 24th', all PRO WO 95/2368.

55. Chalmers, *A Saga of Scotland*, pp 59-60.

56. Ibid, pp 60.

57. Major Rowan, 'Report on the situation of a party of the 97th Inf. Bde...', 21 November 1916, PRO WO 95/2368.

58. Chalmers, *A Saga of Scotland*, pp 62-4, 161.

59. 16th HLI : War Diary, November 1916, PRO WO 95/2403 ; 11th Border Regiment : War Diary, November 1916, PRO WO 95/2403 ; Haig Diary, 21 November 1916, PRO WO 256/14. Haig recorded that Gough was 'very pleased' to have Barnes as Rycroft's successor ; Major-

General R W R Barnes to V Corps, 22 November 1916, 'Report on attempt to relieve a party in dugouts in Frankfort Trench...Night of 21st/22nd November 1916', PRO WO 95/2368. See also 'Report on Operations carried out by the 32nd Division from Nov. 19th to 24th', PRO WO 95/2368.

60. Chalmers, op cit, pp 64-5.

61. 'Report on attack carried out by 16th Lancs. Fus. and 2nd R. Innis. Fus. on 23.11.16. to relieve party in Frankfort Trench', forwarded by Major-General Barnes to V Corps headquarters with a covering note, PRO WO 95/2368 ; 'Report on Operations carried out by the 32nd Division from Nov. 19th to 24th', PRO WO 95/2368.

62. Miles, op cit, footnote 1, p 523.

63. Chalmers, op cit, pp 65-7.

64. Ibid, p 67. Chalmers states that the survivors were awarded one Distinguished Service Order, eleven Distinguished Conduct Medals and twenty-two Military Medals, although he does not make it clear whether these were merely the decorations conferred upon members of the 16th HLI.

65. Girdwood to Edmonds, 30 June 1930, PRO CAB 45/134. Major-General C D Shute commanded the 32nd Division from February to May 1917 and again from June 1917 until April 1918. Lieutenant-Colonel A E McNamara was GSO1 from November 1916 to September 1918. Brigadier-General F W Lumsden, who won the Victoria Cross in April 1917, commanded the 14th Brigade from April 1917 until he was killed on 4 June 1918.

66. See, for instance, Prior and Wilson, *Command on the Western Front*, and also their article 'What Manner of Victory? Reflections on the Termination of the First World War', in *Revue Internationale d'Histoire Militaire*, No. 72, 1990, pp 80-96; Bill Rawling. Surviving Trench Warfare, pp 114-215.

Acknowledgments

I am greatly indebted to my colleagues Suzanne Bardgett, Chris McCarthy and Laurie Milner, and also to John Lee, for their help in the preparation of this article, and to Julia Mills for the maps. Extracts from Crown copyright material held in the Public Record Office and elsewhere are reproduced by permission of the Controller of Her Majesty's Stationery Office.

The Imperial War Museum

The Imperial War Museum illustrates and records all aspects of the two world wars and other military operations involving Britain and the Commonwealth since 1914. The Museum, founded in 1917, was established by Act of Parliament in 1920 and has been in its present home (formerly the Bethlem Royal Hospital or Bedlam) since 1936. The Museum has three branches, HMS *Belfast*, Duxford and the Cabinet War Rooms. The Museum also occupies the former All Saints' Hospital, close to the Main Building, which houses a number of reference departments.

Research and Study Facilities

The Museum welcomes approaches from members of the public for research and study purposes. Its resources cover not only naval, military and air operations but also the social, political, economic and artistic aspects of conflict in the twentieth century.

Visitors intending to use the Museum's reference facilities should be aware that material of relevance to their fields of study may be found in more than one of the departments listed below. Separate leaflets describing the holdings of the departments and the services they offer are available on request.

Department of Art: responsible for the Museum's paintings, drawings and sculptures, and for its collections of posters, medallions and postcards. The Department also has a unique collection of correspondence with artists who were commissioned under the war artist scheme in the two world wars.

Department of Documents: primary source material, largely composed of British private papers and captured German records. It includes the papers of high-ranking officers such as Field Marshals Sir John French, Sir Henry Wilson and Viscount Montgomery of Alamein, manuscripts of the war poets and writers Isaac Rosenberg and Siegfried Sassoon and many personal diaries, letters and unpublished memoirs.

Department of Exhibits and Firearms: administers the Museum's collections of three-dimensional objects. Besides such larger exhibits as aircraft, artillery, vehicles and small craft, most of which are displayed at Duxford near Cambridge, the holdings include uniforms, insignia, weapons, flags, communications equipment, models, medical equipment, cameras, toys, currency and ephemera.

Department of Film: holds more than forty million feet of film. Apart from material shot by service cameramen and films sponsored by the service ministries and the Ministry of Information, there are substantial holdings from other Allied and enemy sources, as well as many important documentaries, television compilations and feature films.

Department of Photographs: a national archive of some five million photographs which includes the work of official military, professional and private photographers. Guides to various areas of the collection include a concise catalogue covering the First and Second World Wars. Lists of photographs on specific subjects are available and a catalogue of their titles can be sent on request.

Department of Printed Books: a national reference library comprising over 100,000 books as well as extensive collections of pamphlets, periodicals, maps and technical drawings. In addition the Department holds important special collections including those on women's activities during the First World War, aerial propaganda leaflets and ephemera such as song-sheets, stamps and theatre programmes.

Department of Sound Records: over 15,000 hours of recorded material, retrospective interviews with service personnel and civilians, contemporary archive recordings including speeches by well known personalities, war reports and broadcasts, sound effects and war crimes trials; and miscellaneous recordings such as radio programmes, lectures and poetry readings.

Opening hours

Reference Departments
Monday to Friday 10.00 am to 5.00 pm

At least 24 hours' notice should be given of an intended visit (for a visit to the Department of Art at least 48 hours' notice, and for the Department of Film at least one week's notice is necessary).

Saturday 10.00 am to 5.00 pm

Departments of Documents and Printed Books only. A restricted service is offered on Saturday (except Bank Holiday weekends and the last two weekends of November). An appointment is essential since only pre-booked material can be made available and there is limited seating.

The Reference Departments are closed on Bank Holidays. The Departments of Documents and Printed Books are closed for the last two full weeks in November.

Imperial War Museum, Lambeth Road
London SE1 6HZ 0171-416 5000

Back numbers of the Imperial War Museum Review are available from:

> Mail Order,
> Imperial War Museum,
> Duxford, Cambridge, CB2 4QR.

Payment must be made in sterling, either by international money order or a cheque drawn on a UK clearing bank. Access, Visa and Mastercard are also accepted. Telephone: 01223 835000 X245. Fax: 01223 837267. Details of trade information available on 0171 416 5396.

Review No 3 (published 1988)

'A wonderful idea of the fighting': the question of fakes in The Battle of the Somme

The evacuation of Cape Helles, Gallipoli

Kamp Kufstein: a record of international refugee work in Austria during 1945

'Vive La Nation': French revolutionary themes in the posters and prints of the First World War

Night for day: the symbolic value of light in the painting of the Second World War

JW.53: convoy to Russia

'The Dead Man's Penny': a history of the Next of Kin memorial plaque

The Japanese Long Lance torpedo and its place in naval history

'Swingmusik is verboten': official policy towards popular music and 'dissident' youth in the Third Reich

'You smug-faced crowds': poetry on the Home Front in the First World War

'I know what it is to kill a pig; I won't kill a man': the Museum's oral history programme on conscientious objectors of the First World War

Change: some military consequences following the demise of our Indian Empire (by Colonel Brian Montgomery)

Review No 4 (published 1989)

Olive Edis: Imperial War Museum photographer in France and Belgium, March 1919

An introduction to the papers of Field Marshal Sir Henry Wilson

Images of war in Italy: the record made by the Army Film and Photgraphic Unit in Emilia Romagna, 1944-1945

An appreciation of the shelter photographs taken by Bill Brandt in November 1940

Moving images? The Parliamentary Recruiting Committee's poster campaign, 1914-1916

Des Illusions … Désillusions: an introduction to parties, personalities and posters in collaborationist France, 1940-1944

A gift for Christmas: the story of Princess Mary's Gift Fund, 1914

The German 'Biber' submarine

The trench raid at Chérisy, 15 September 1917

The loss of HMS *Hood*, 24 May 1941

The Ministry of Information and documentary film, 1939-1945

Review No 5 (published 1990)

Women in Munitions 1914-1918: the oral record

The Open Exhaust and some other trench journals of The First World War

The Liberation of Bergen-Belsen concentration camp in April 1945: the testimony of those involved

Henry Lamb and the First World War

'…And, if necessary, to carry it out': Operation Sealion and the Black Book, fact and fiction

Small arms of Nationalist China 1937-1945

Film and reality: the *San Demetrio* episode

West Indians in Britain during the Second World War: a short history drawing on Colonial Office papers

The controversy over the use of the dum dum bullets in the First World War

Review No 6 (published 1991)

Military mining on the Western Front

The writings of A B Austin, *Daily Herald* war correspondent

The First World War Women's Work Collection

The ethos of the British High Command, 1914-1918

Wyndham Lewis's war pictures

Bomber Command in the Battle of Britain

Christian iconography and First World War memorials

Americans in the Royal Flying Corps

Maurice Chevalier and charges of collaboration

Review No 7 (published 1992)

Army photographers in North-West Europe

Two Fusiliers: the First World War friendship of Robert Graves and Siegfried Sassoon

War propaganda and fascist myth: the poster collections of the Micheletti Foundation, Brescia

Early paintings of the Great War

'Keep smiling, keep those chins up and God Bless': filmed messages home from service personnel in the Far East during the Second World War

Post-war reconstruction as depicted in official British films of the Second World War

'Large Slow Targets': the Royal Navy's LST (2) Fleet in the Second World War

'The Number One Radio Personality of the War': Lord Haw Haw and his British audience during the Phoney War

The inevitable victory? El Alamein revisited

'The drama of the larder': Germany's food crisis 1914-1918

'The most lion-hearted man I ever met': Commander J W 'Tubby' Linton VC

Review No 8 (published 1993)

The end of the British Mandate in Palestine: reflections from the papers of John Watson, a member of the Forces Broadcasting Service

The British Pacific Fleet of 1944-45 and its newspaper, *Pacific Post*

'When d'you scarper? When d'you go into action? That's the nightmare!' The destruction of the South Nottinghamshire Hussars at Knightsbridge, 27 May - 6 June 1942

The war art of C R W Nevinson

The empty battlefield: the artist and landscape in the First World War

'Nobody's child': a brief history of the tactical use of Vickers machine-guns in the First World War

Too old or too bold? The removal of Sir Roger Keyes as Churchill's first Director of Combined Operations

Eton and the First World War

The German battlecruiser attack on the east coast ports, 16 December 1914